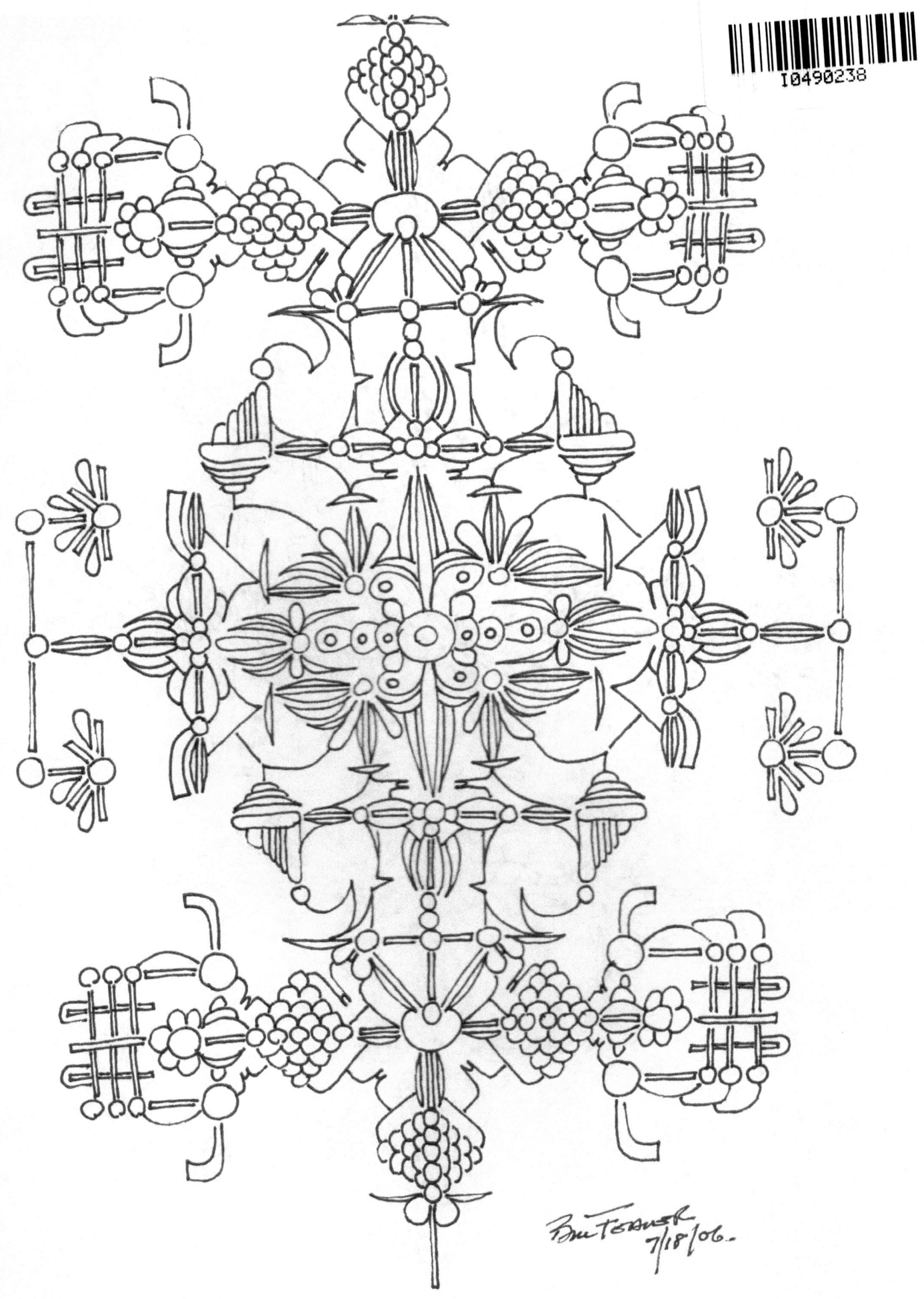

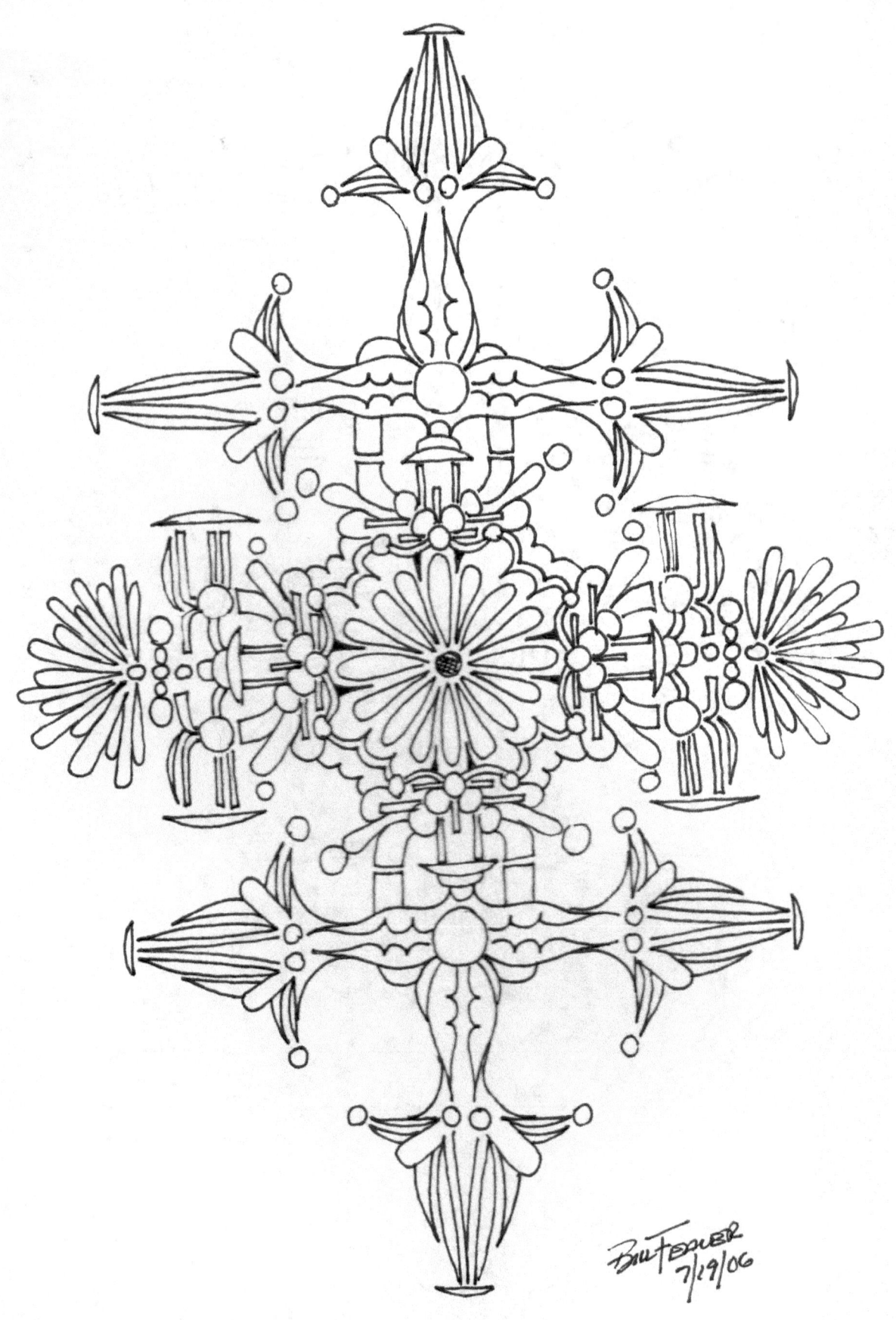

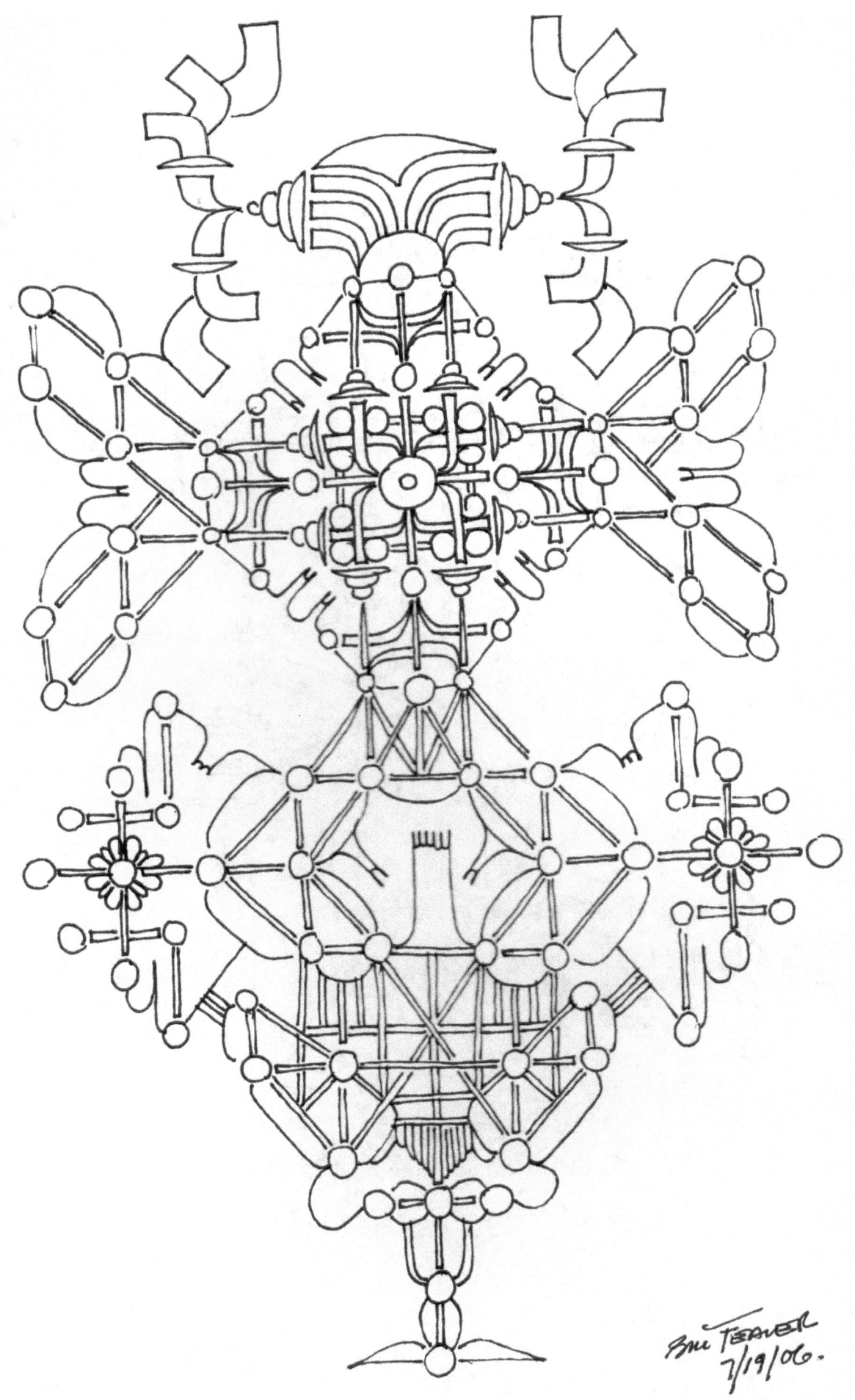

Bru Teaver 7/19/06.

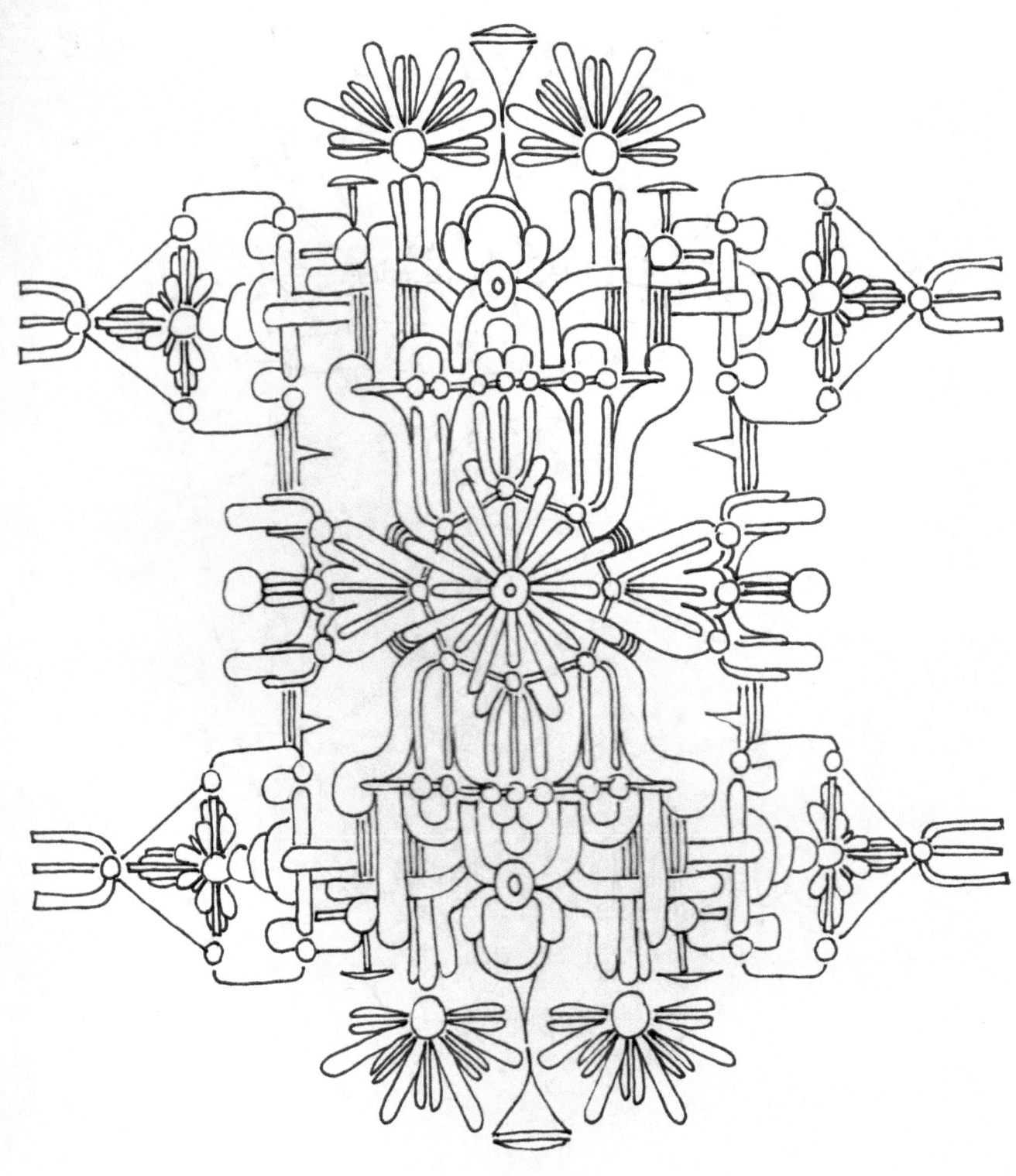

Bill Feather
7-19-06.

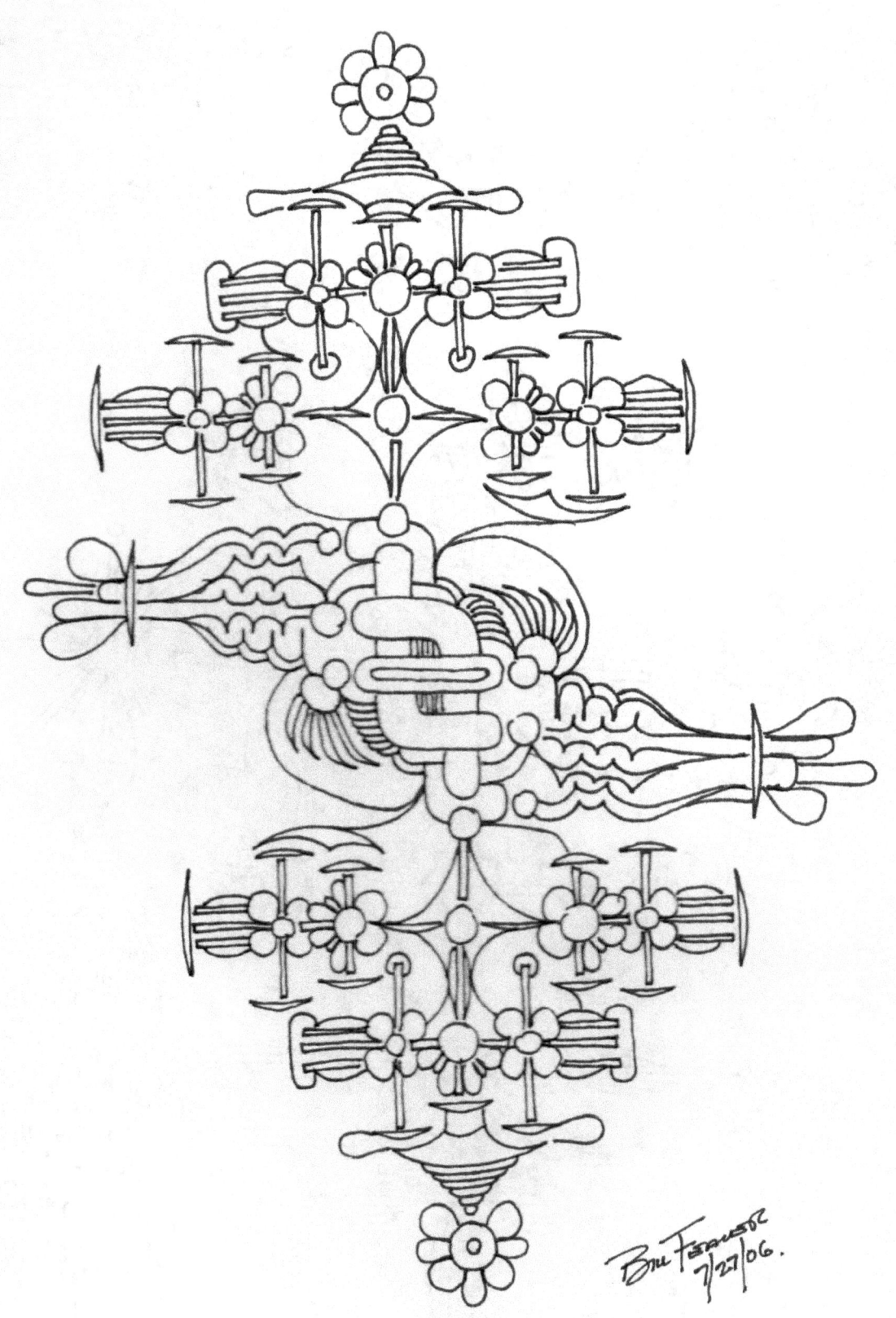

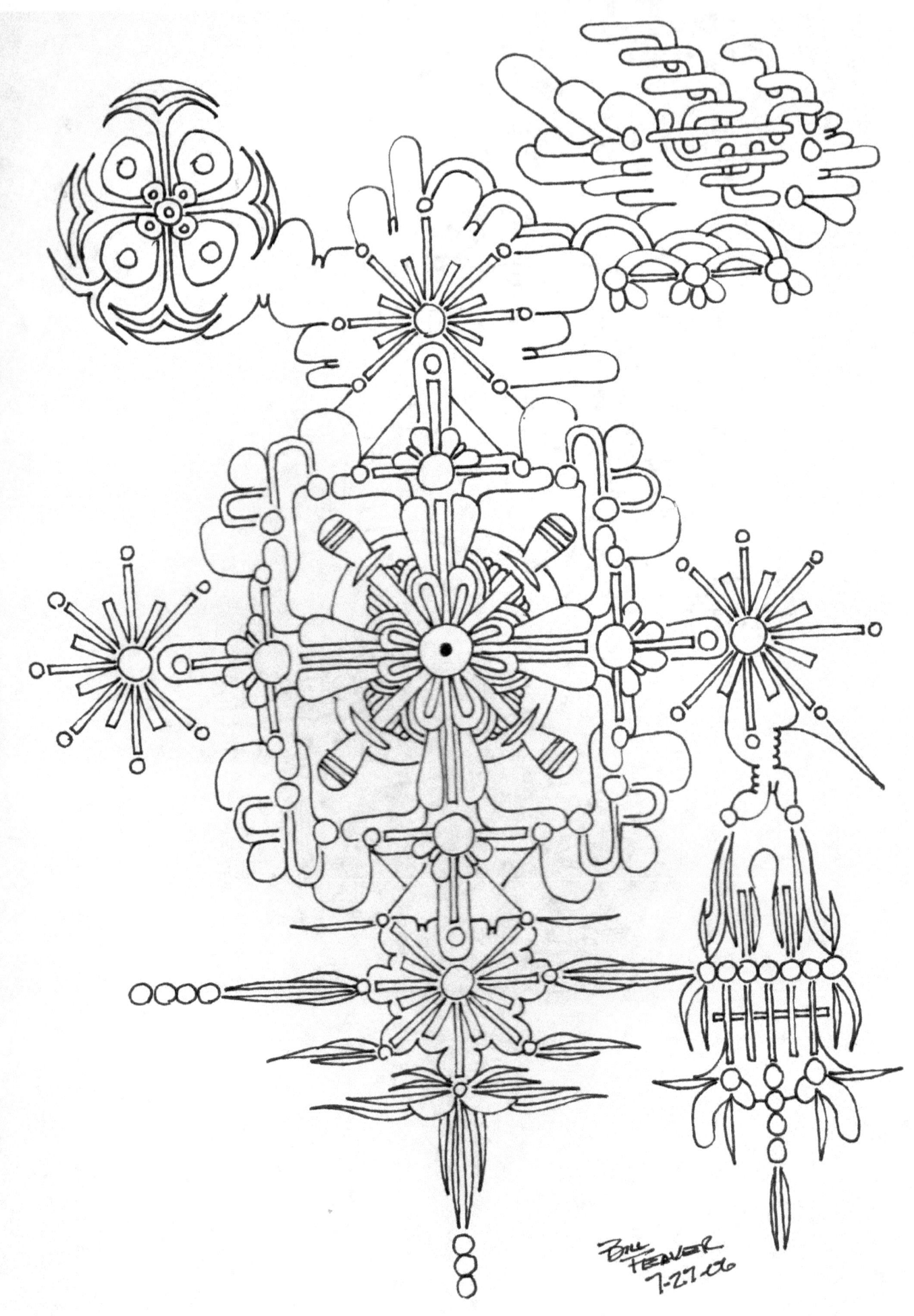

Bill
Feaver
7-27-06

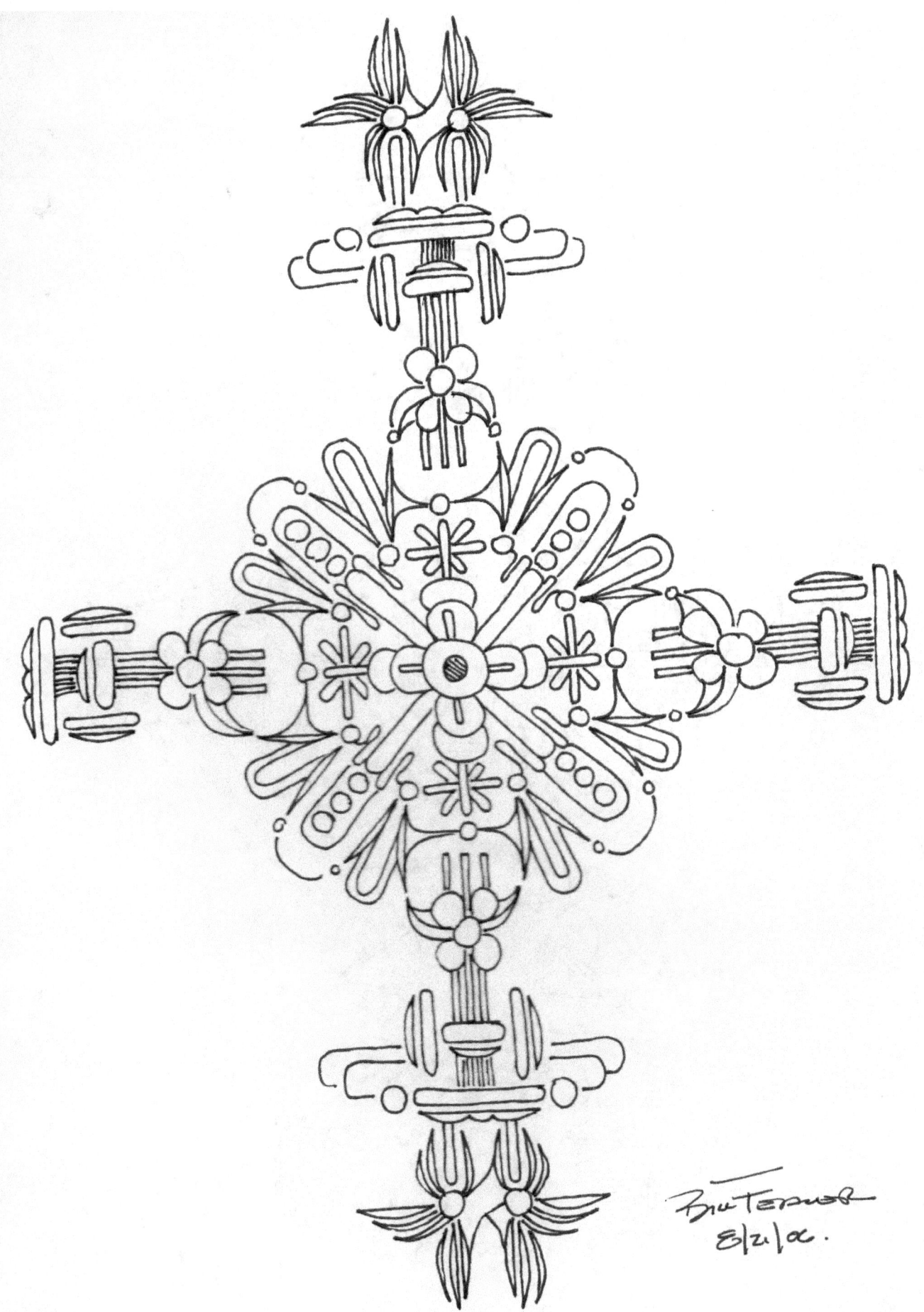

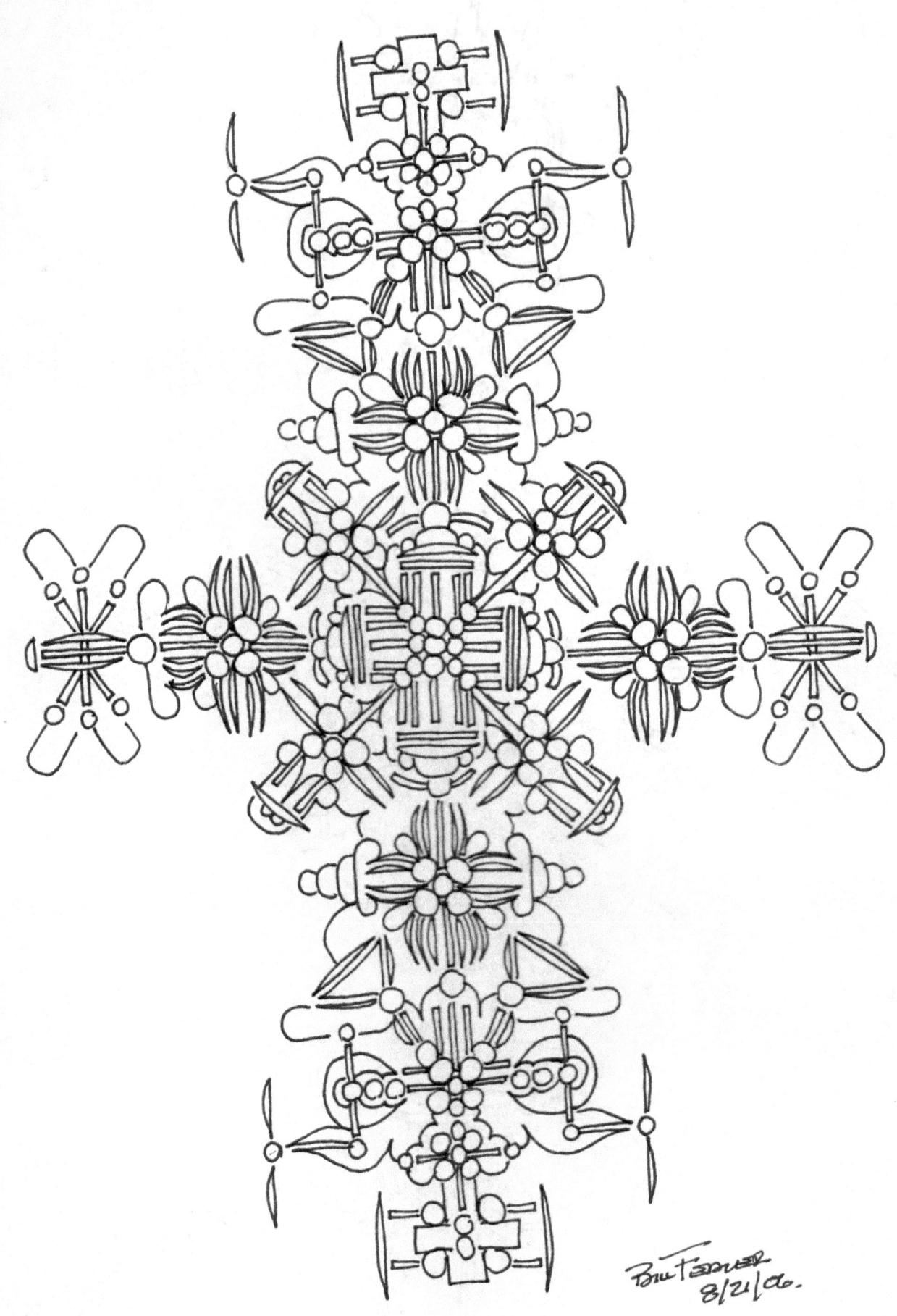

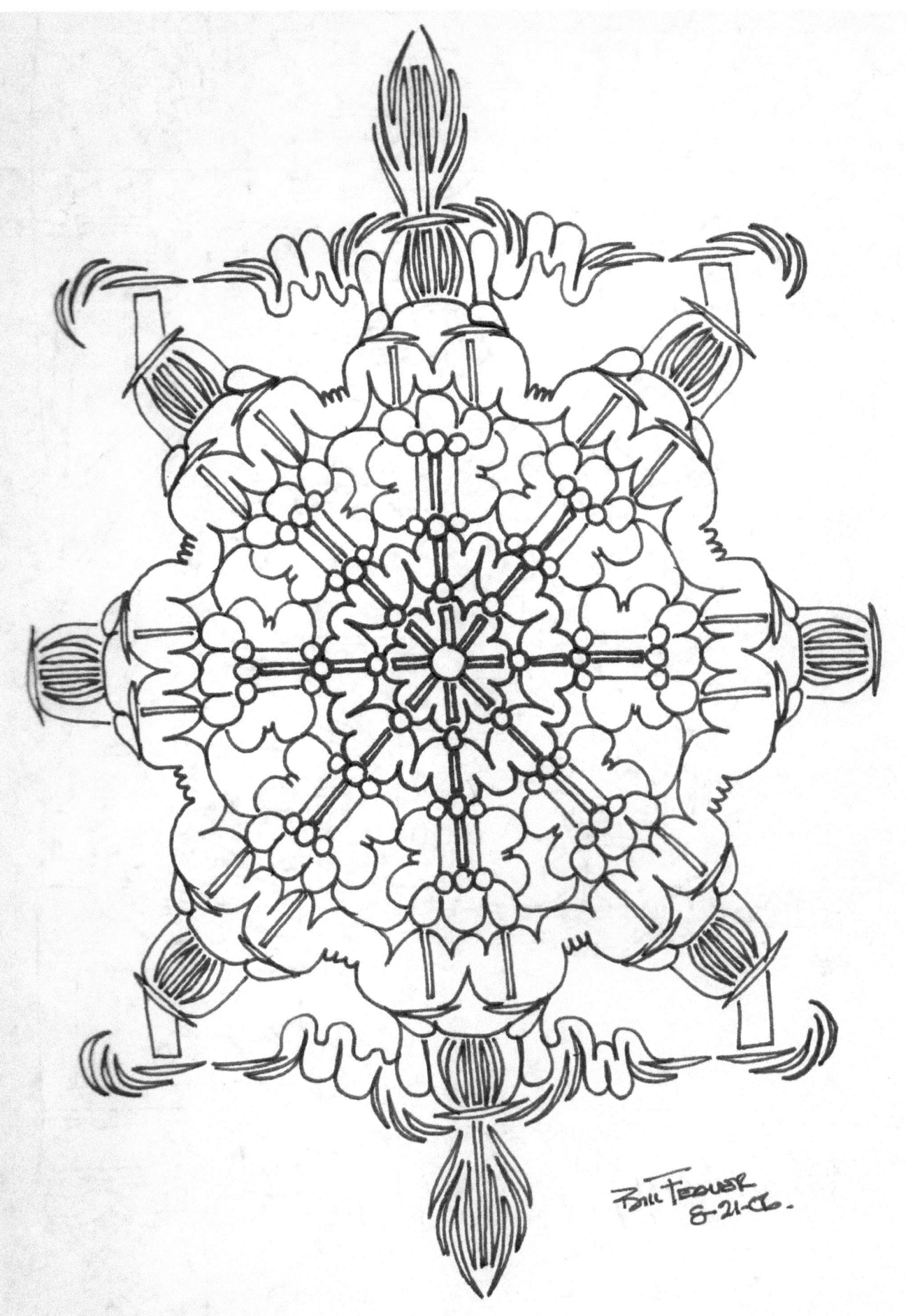

Bill Ferguson
8-21-06.

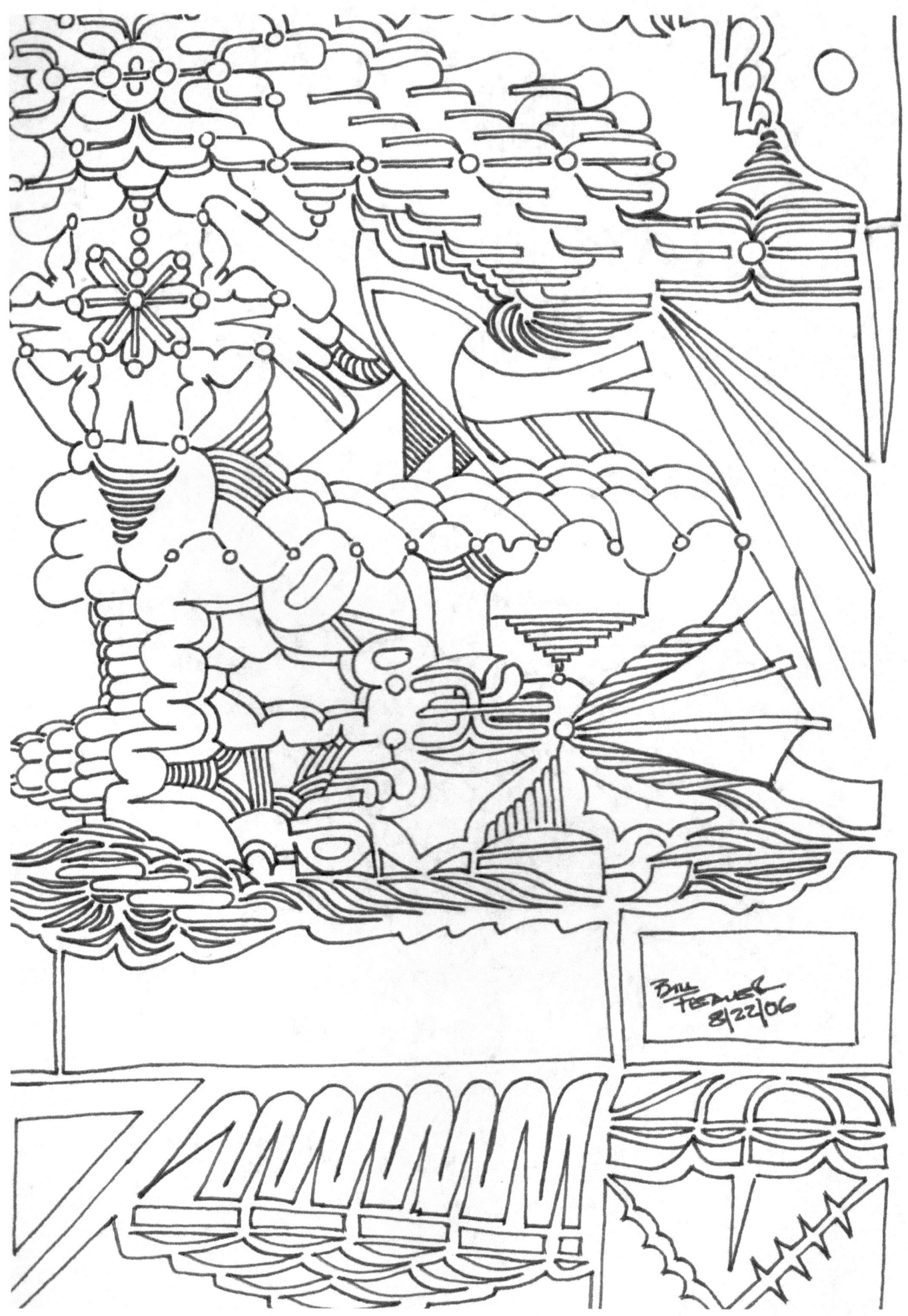

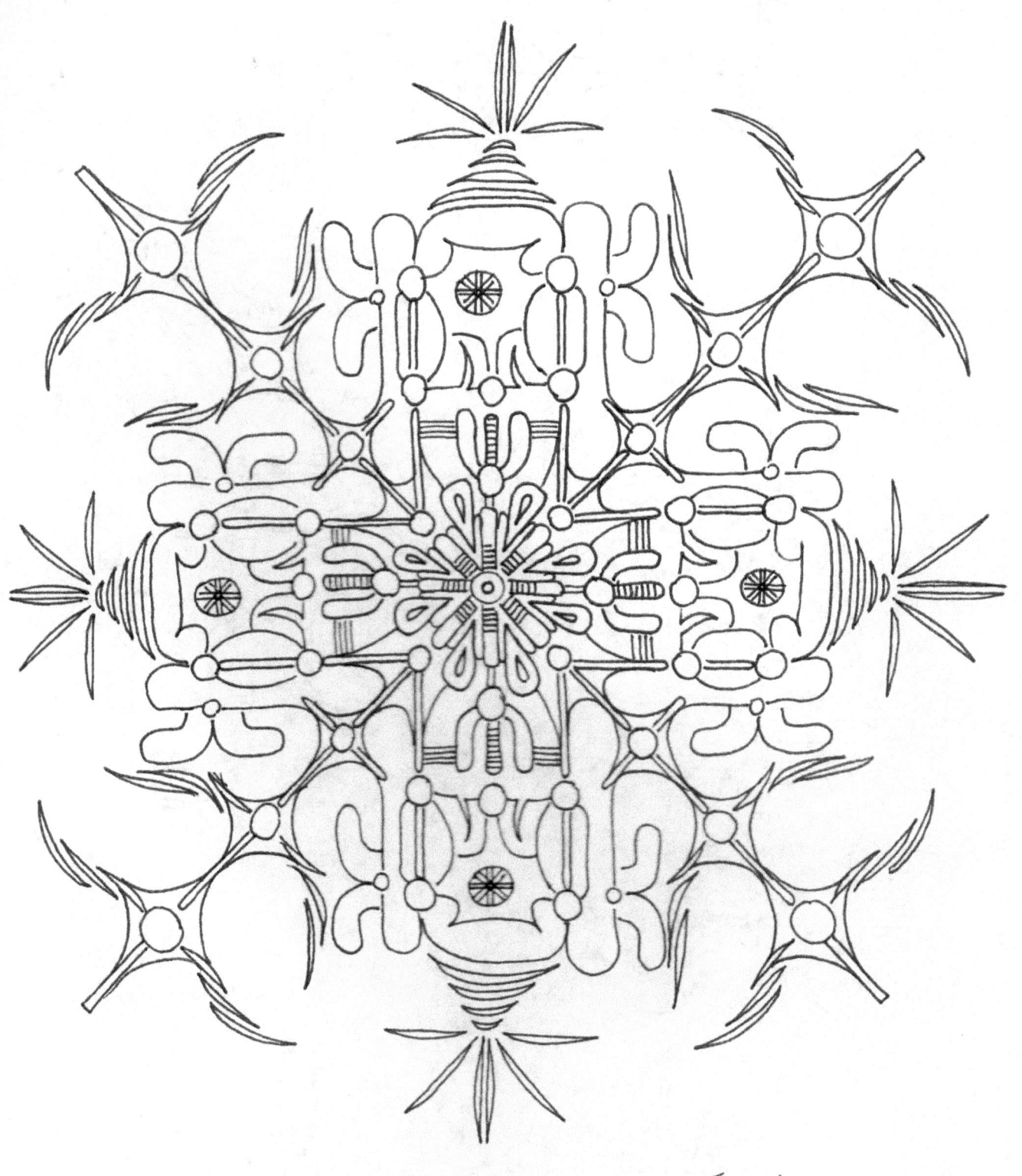

Paul Teanes
8/22/06.

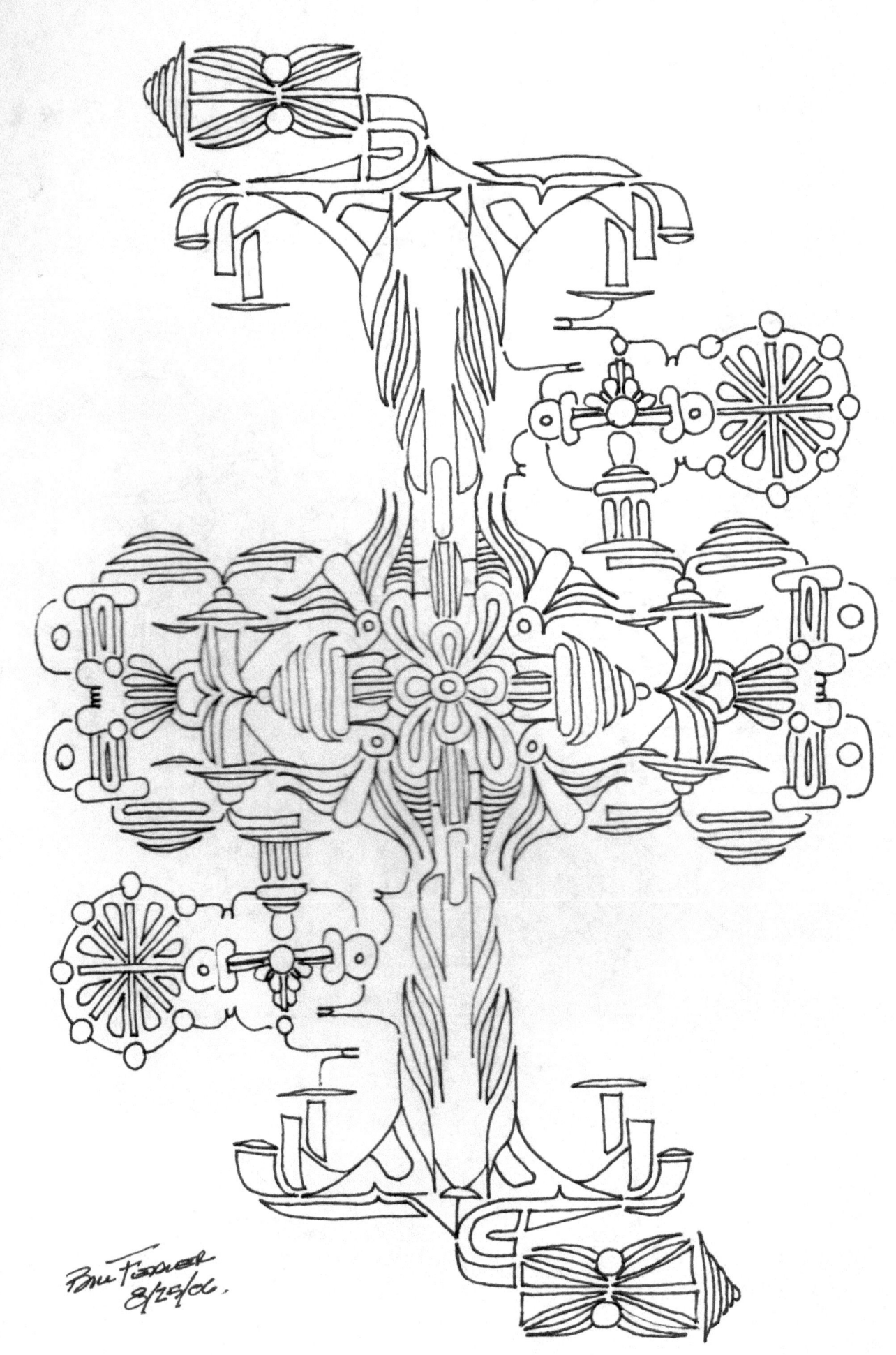

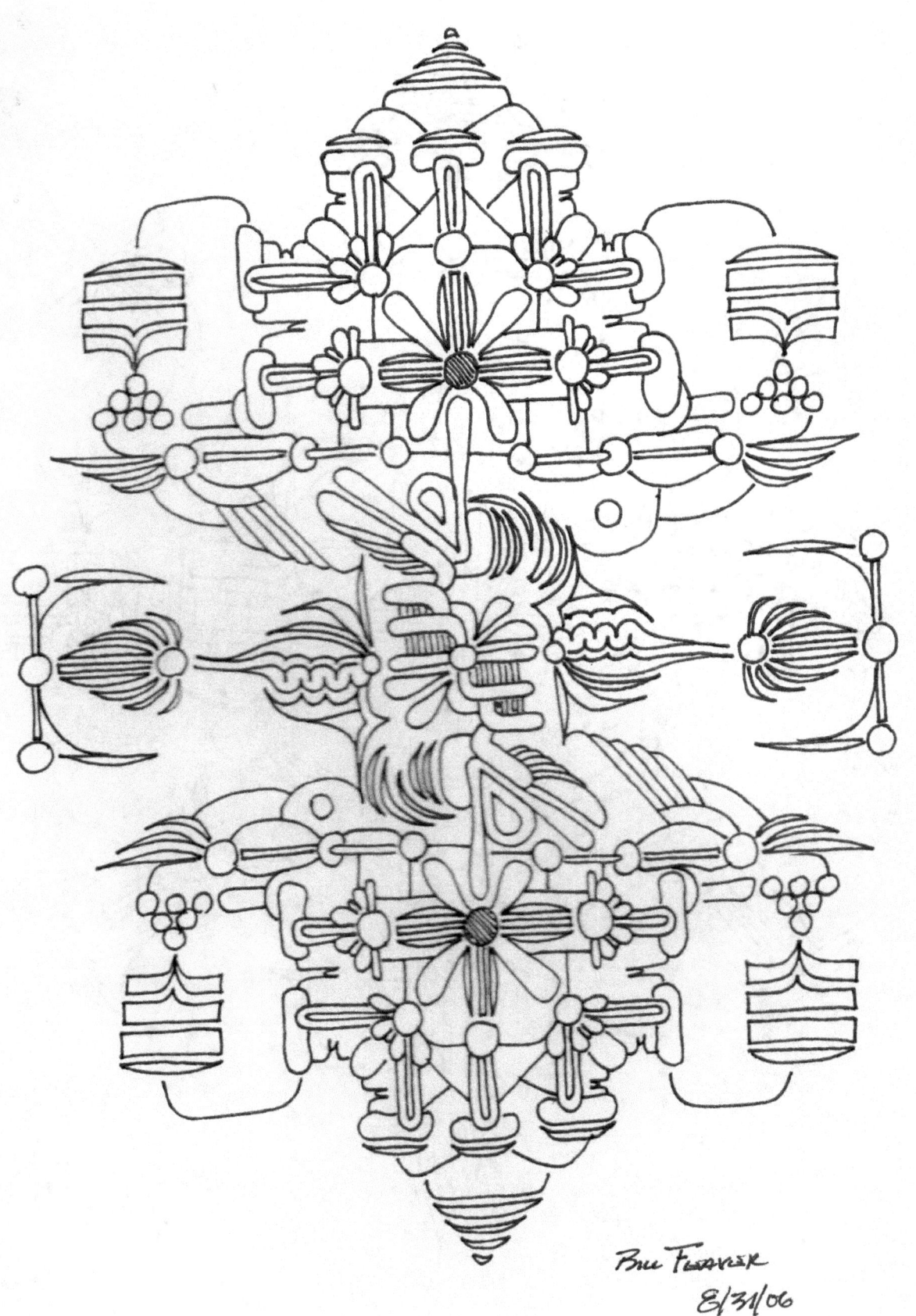

Bill Fleaver
8/31/06

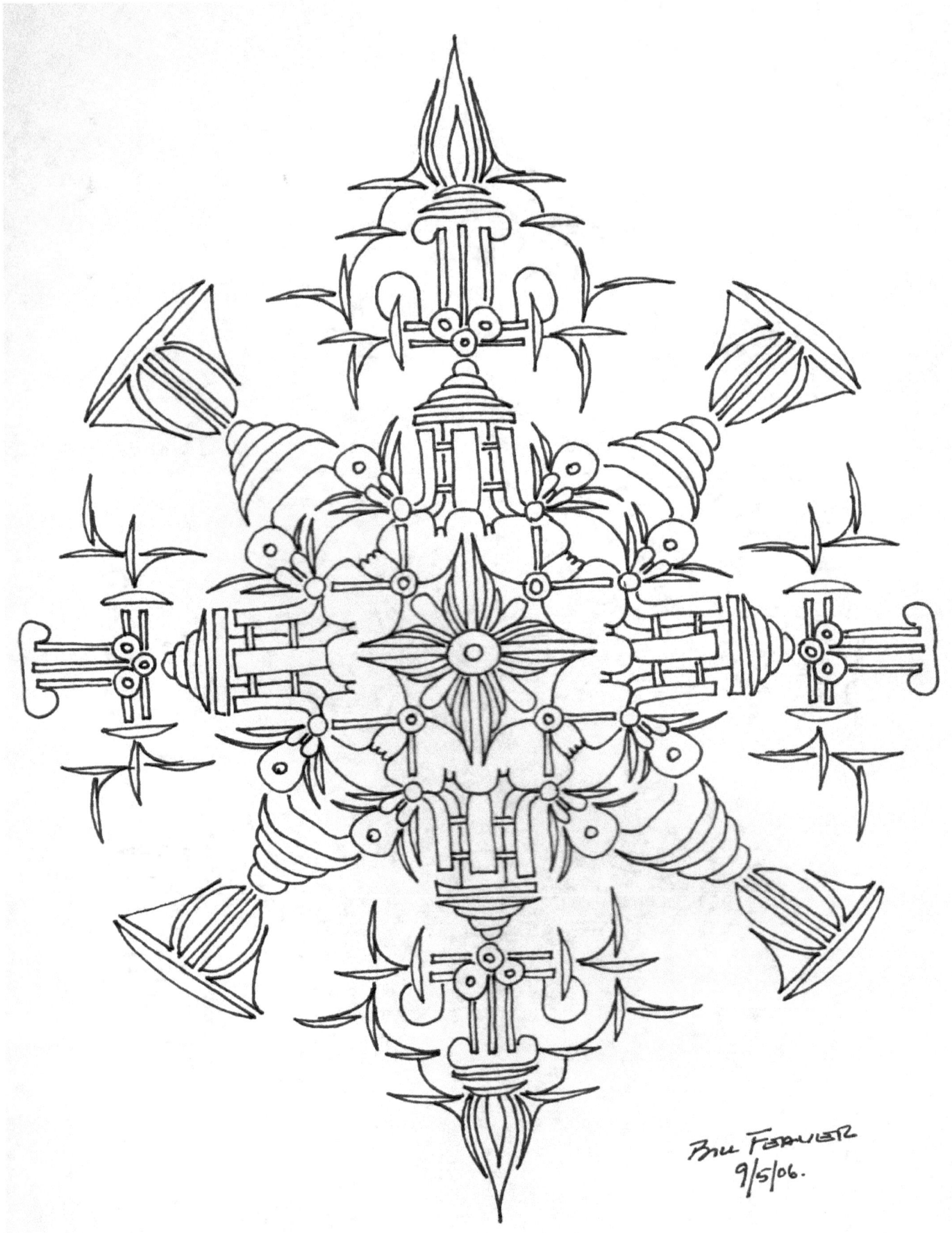

Bill Fesauer
9/5/06.

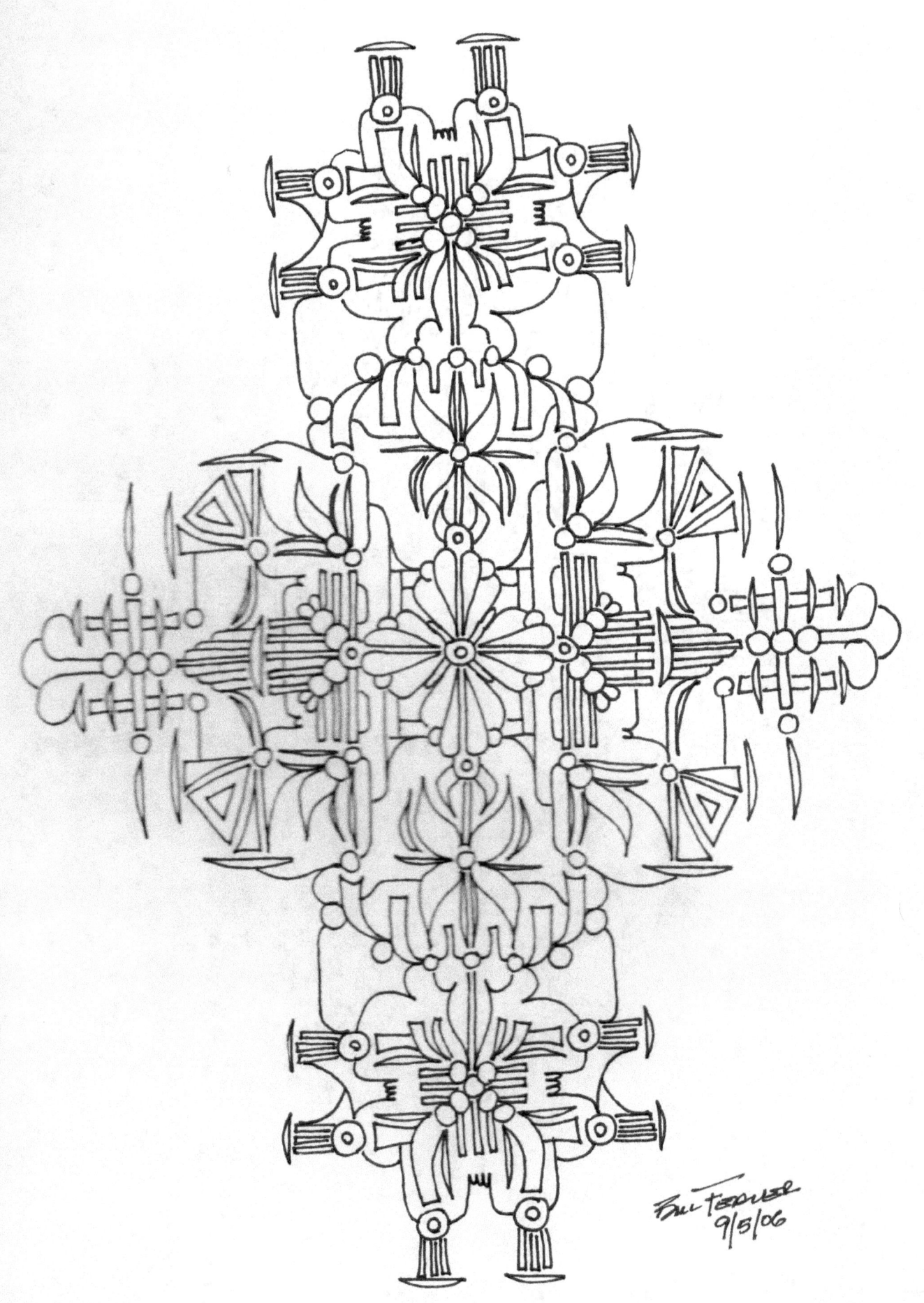

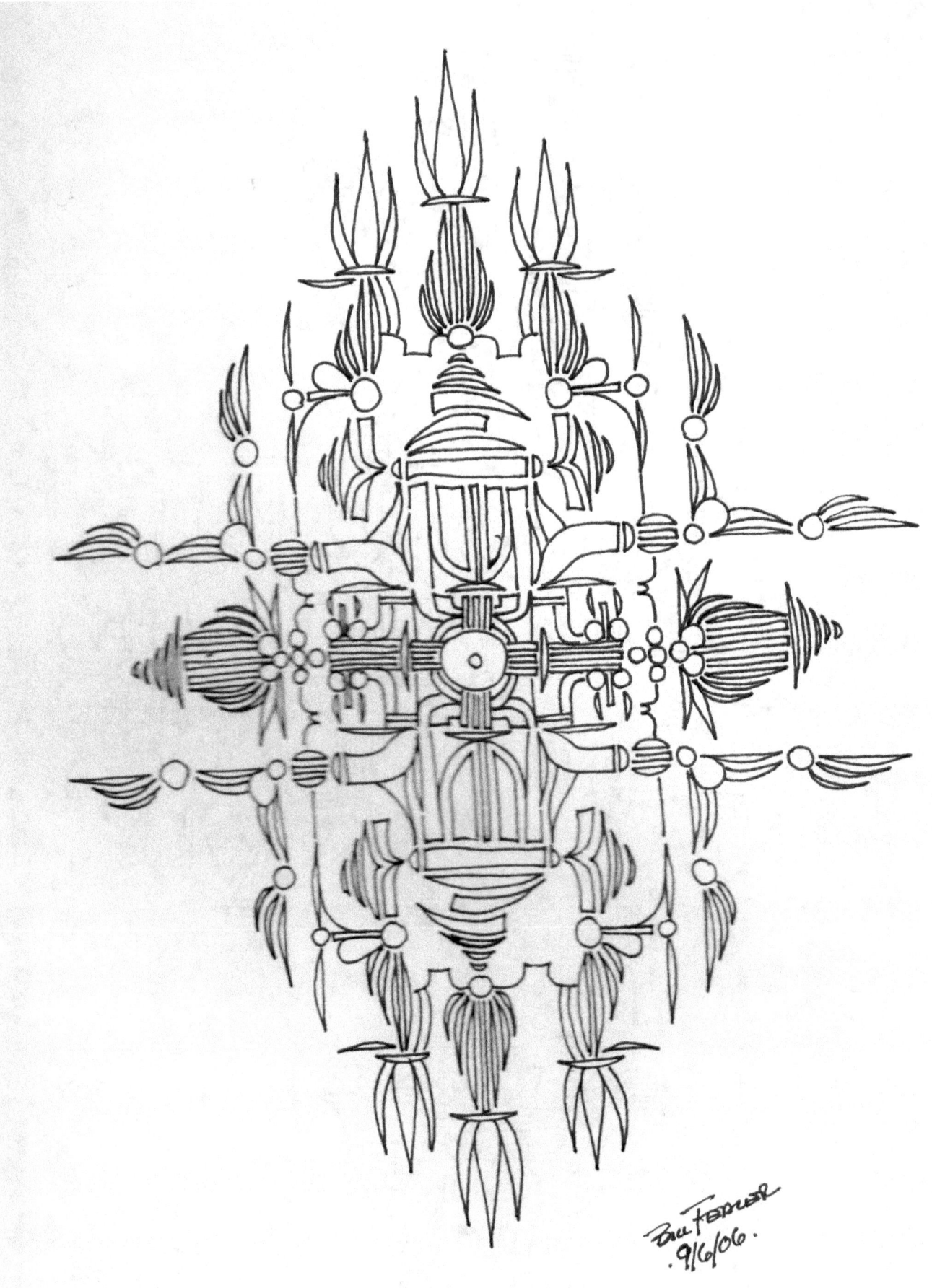

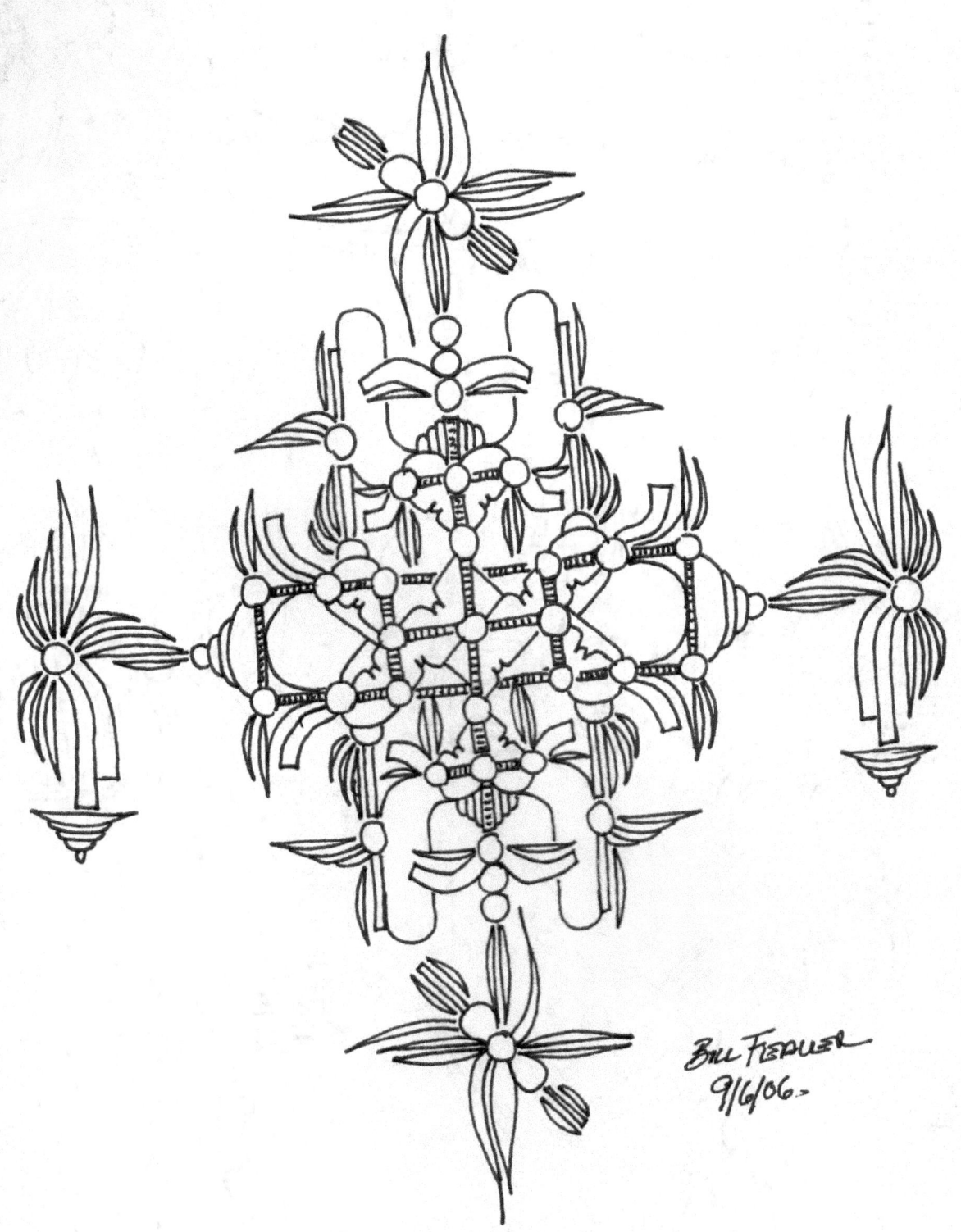

Bill Fiedler
9/6/06.

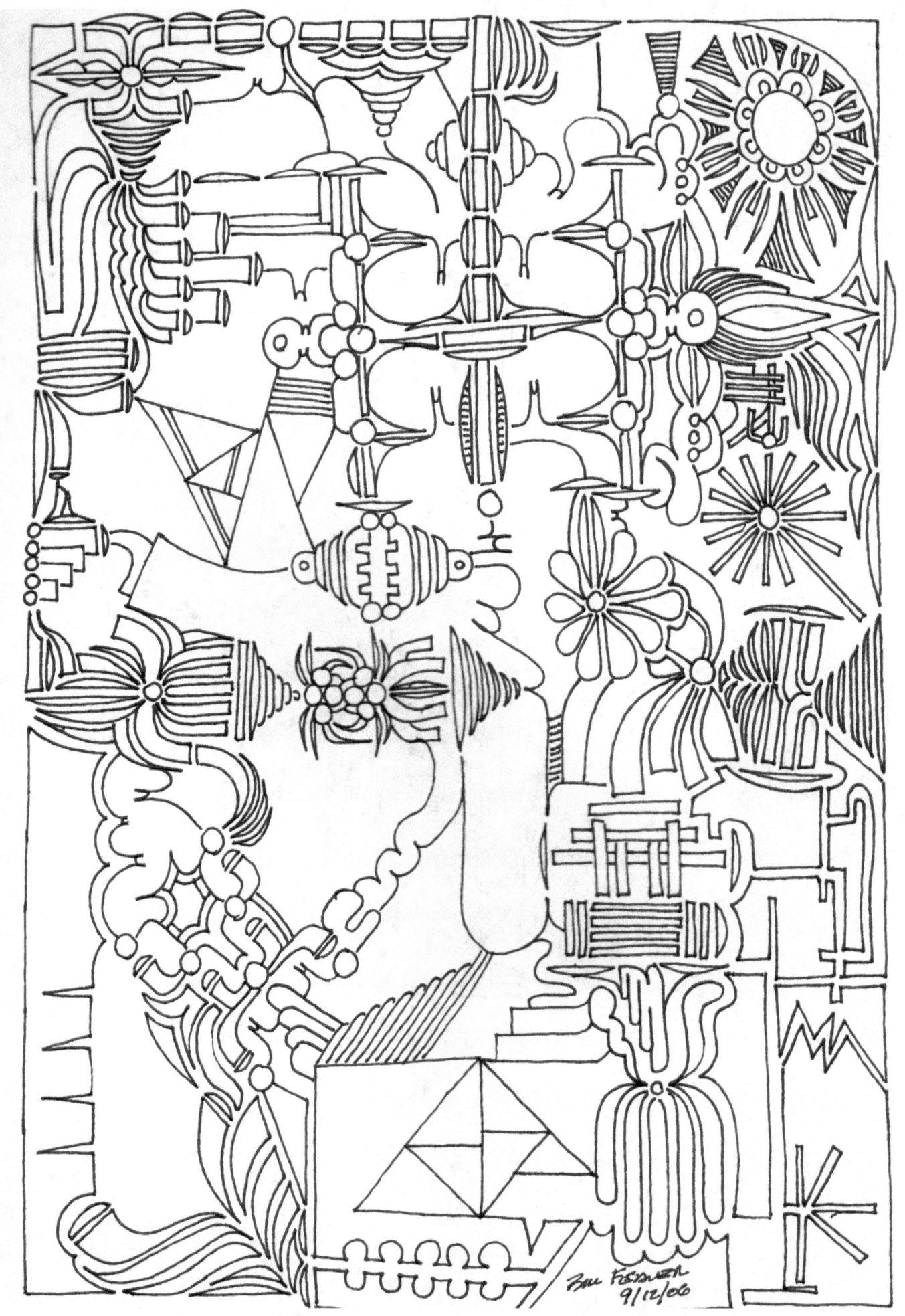

Bill Fessler
9/12/06

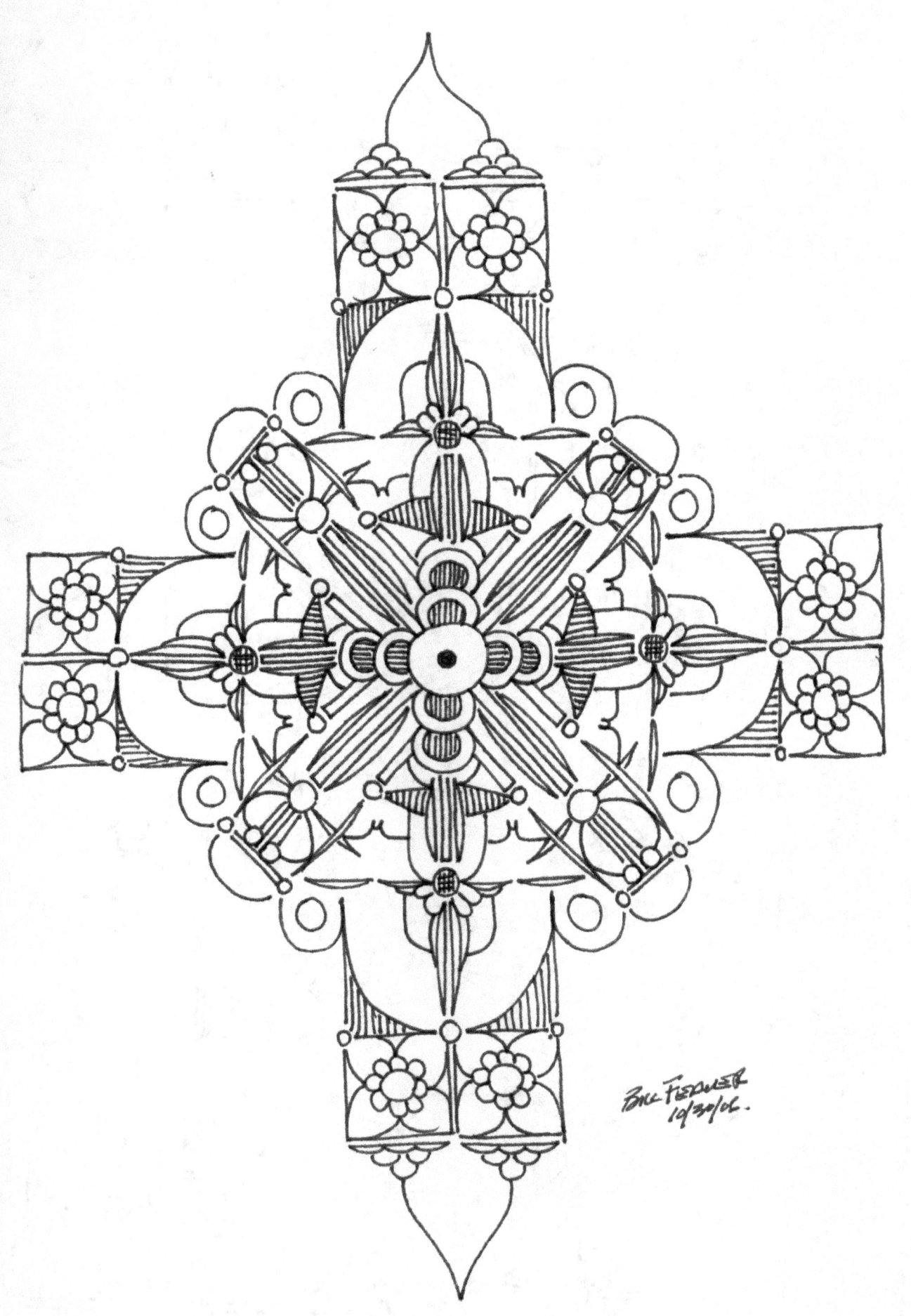

Bill Fedder
10/30/06.

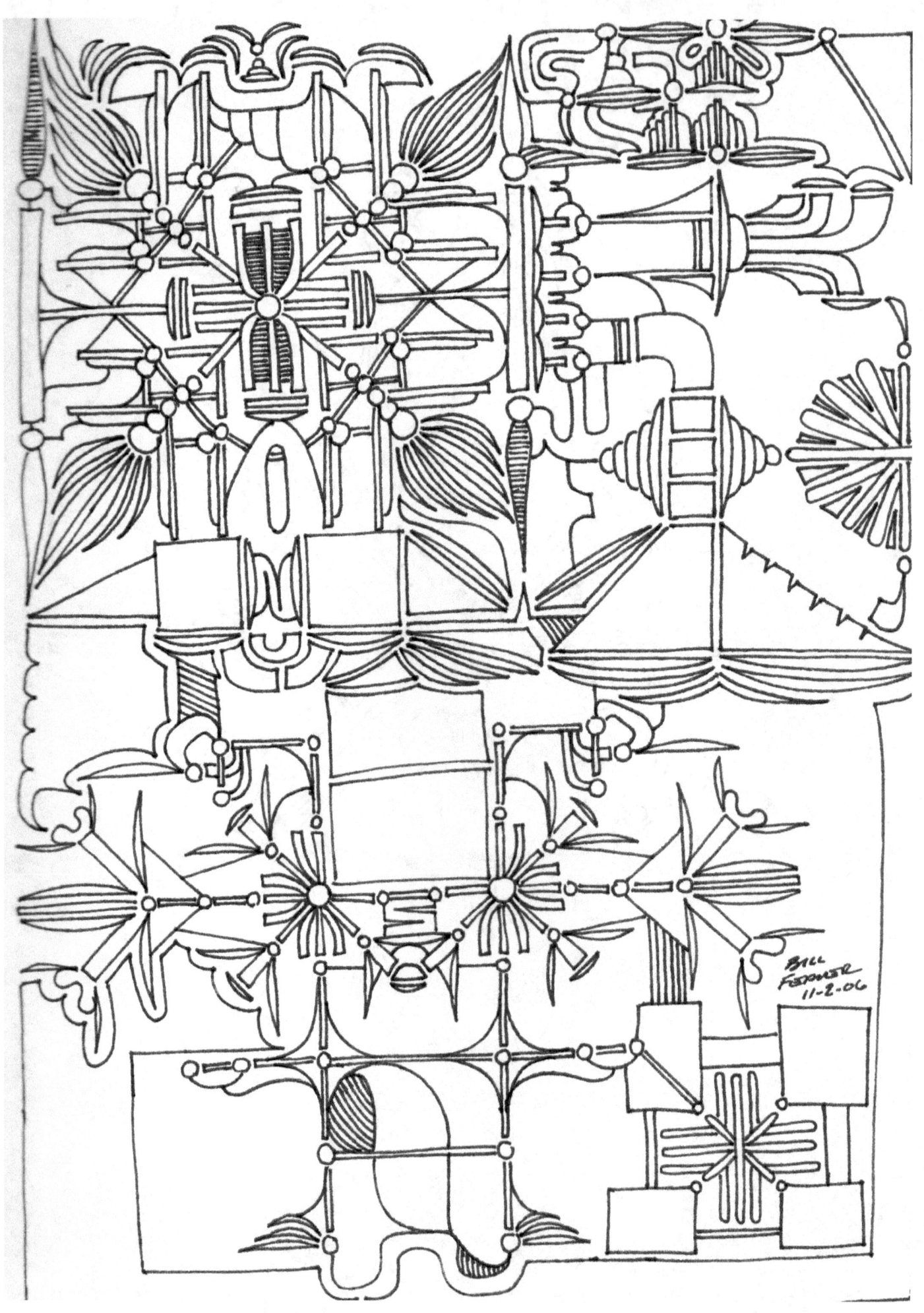

BILL
FERRNER
11-2-06

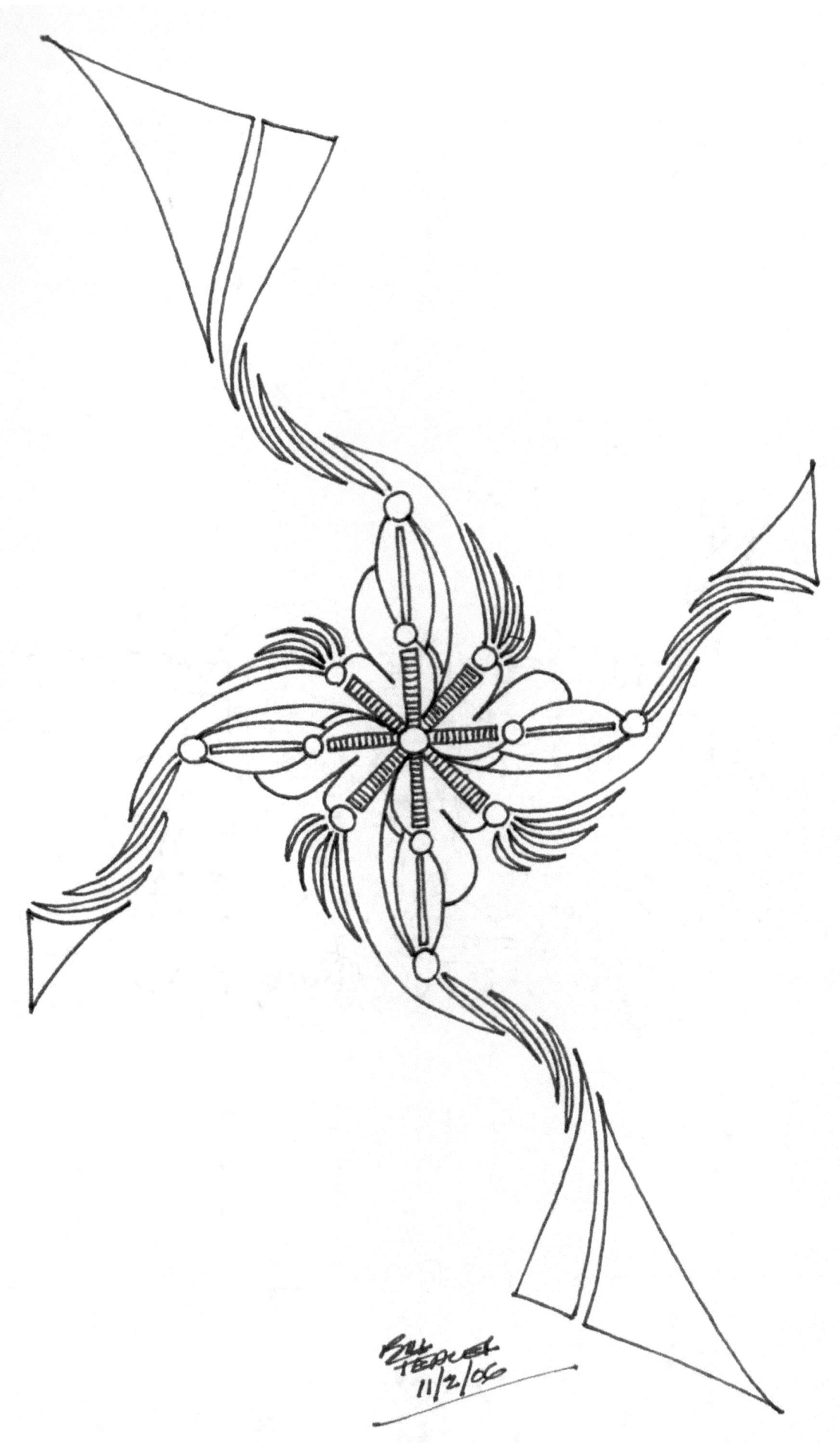

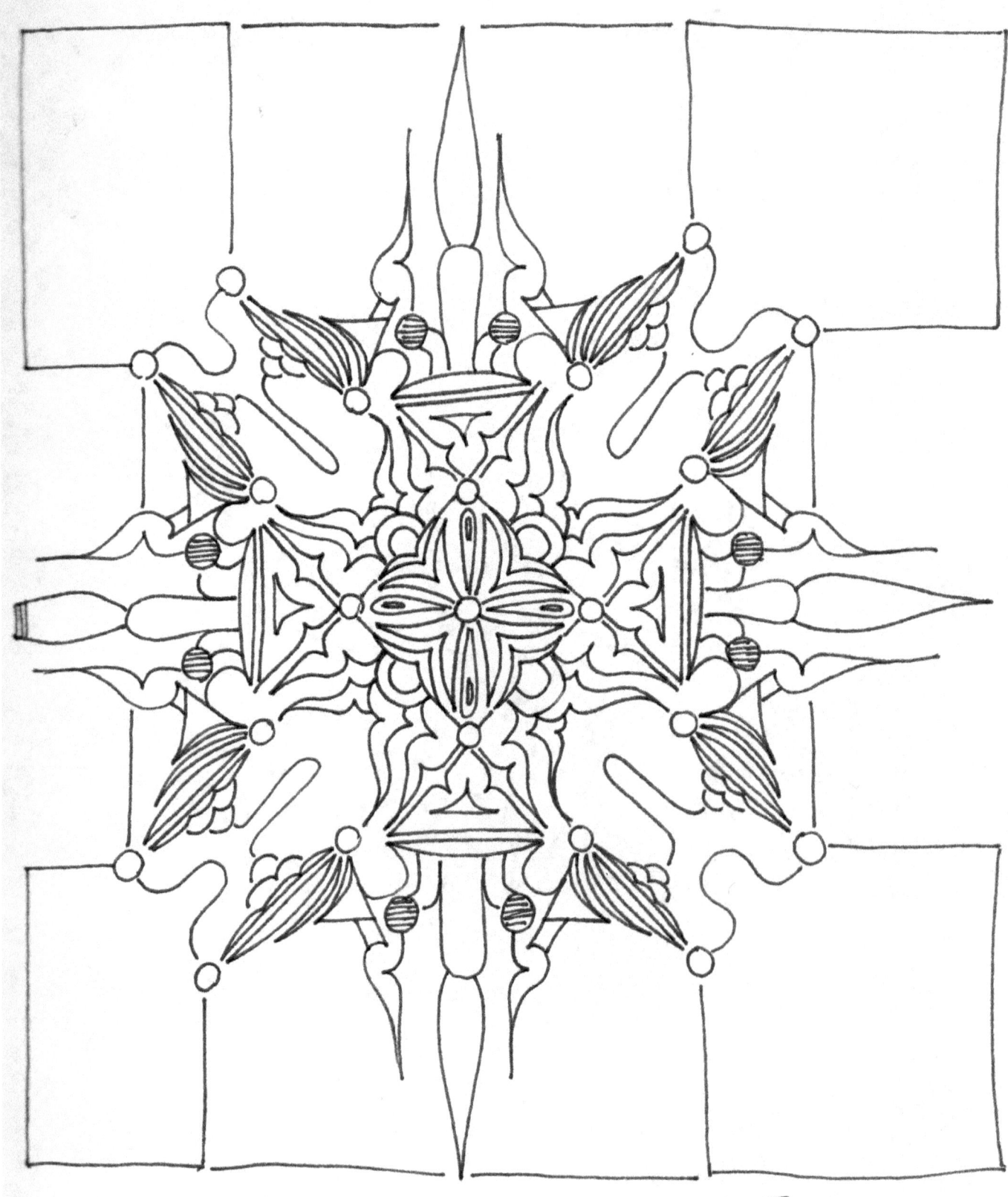

Bill Feaver
11/2/06

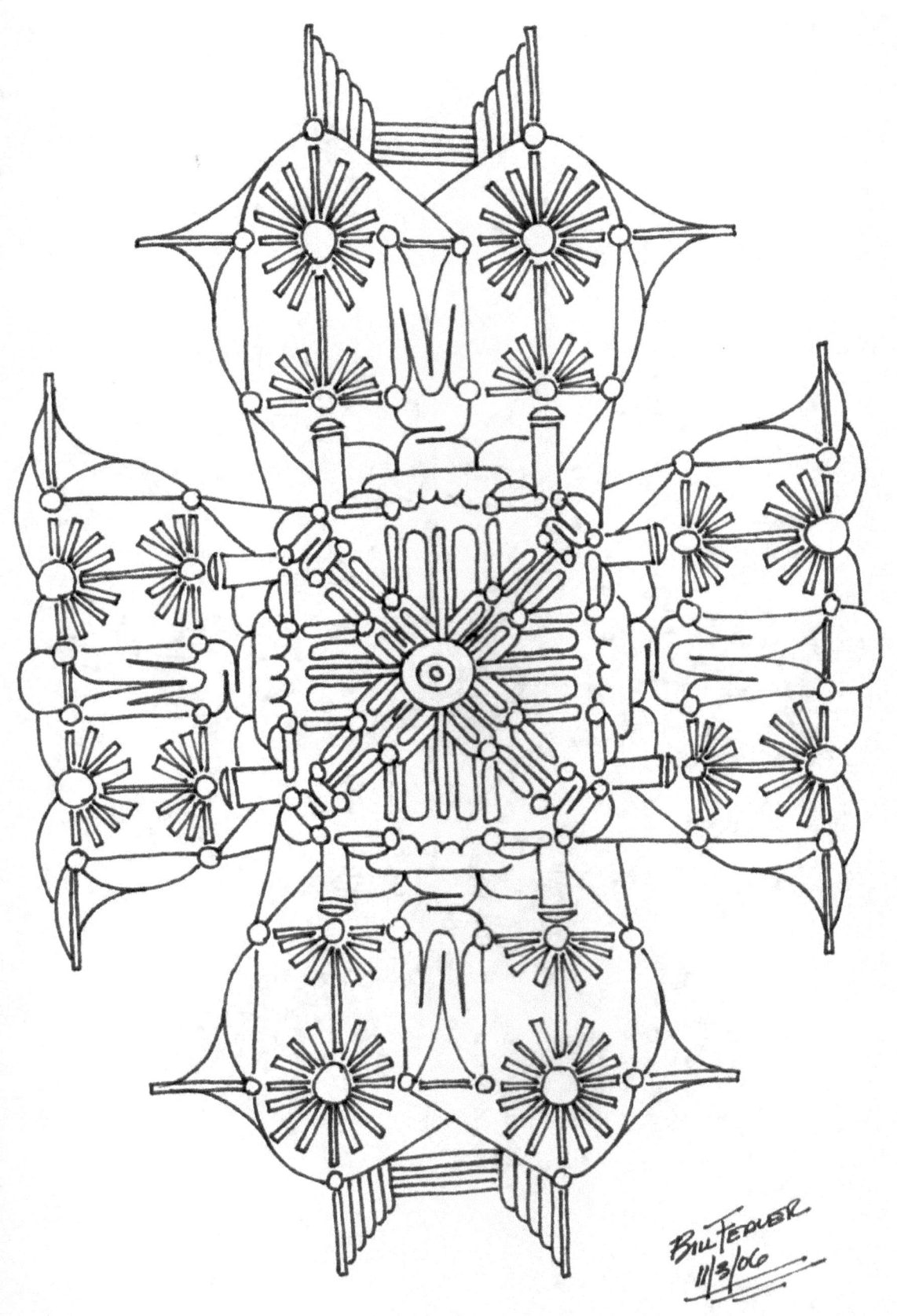

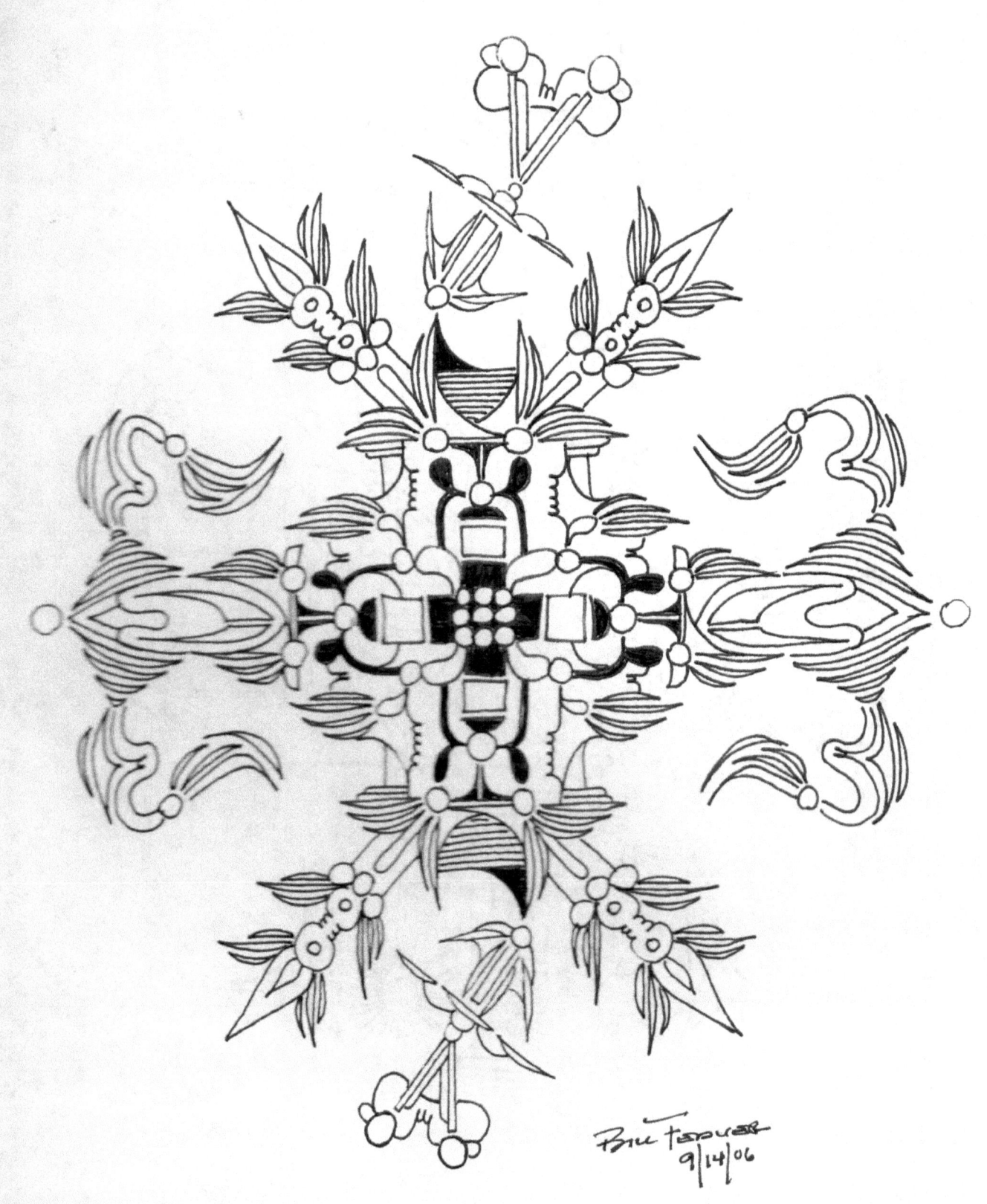

Bill Fessler
9/14/06

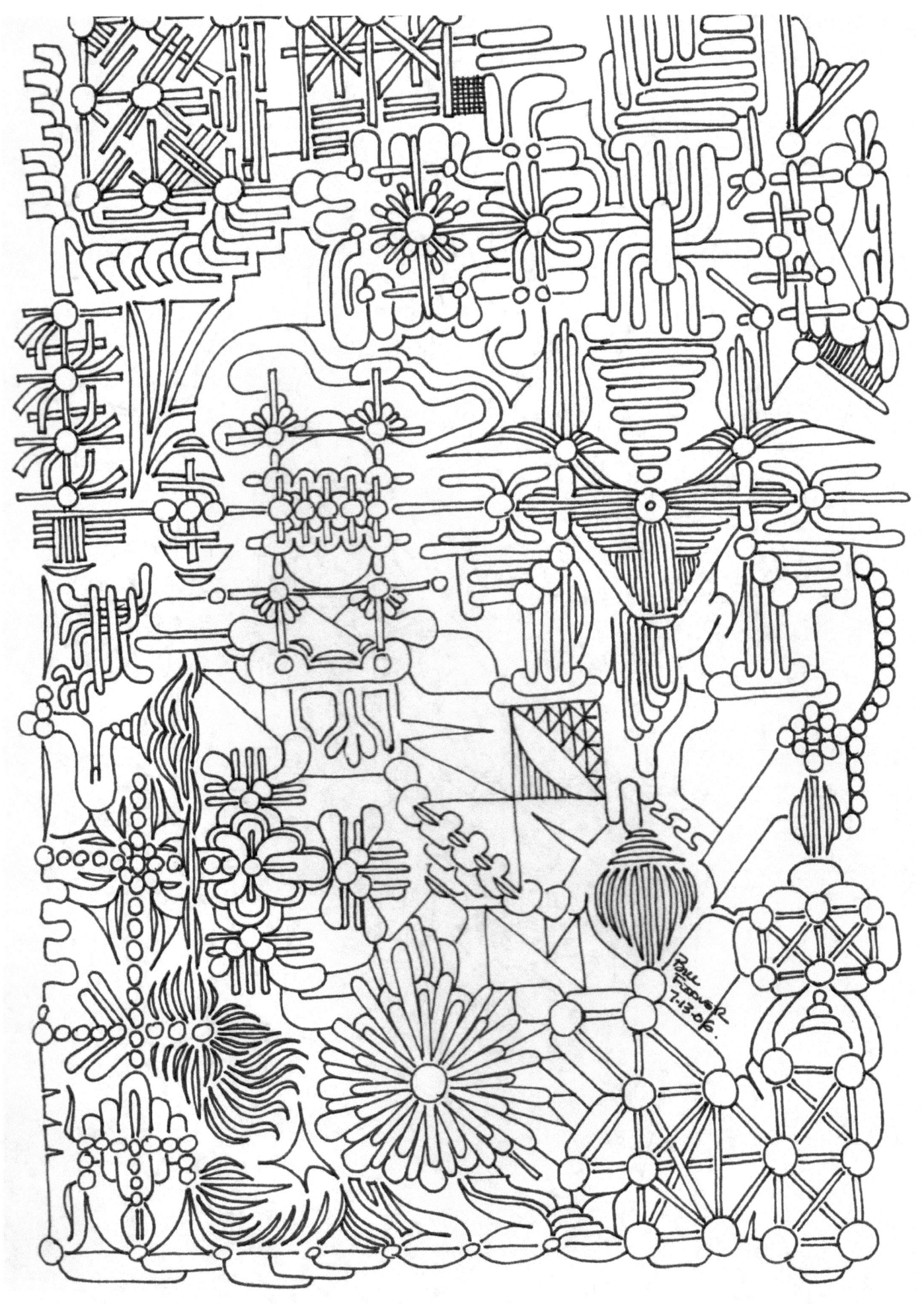

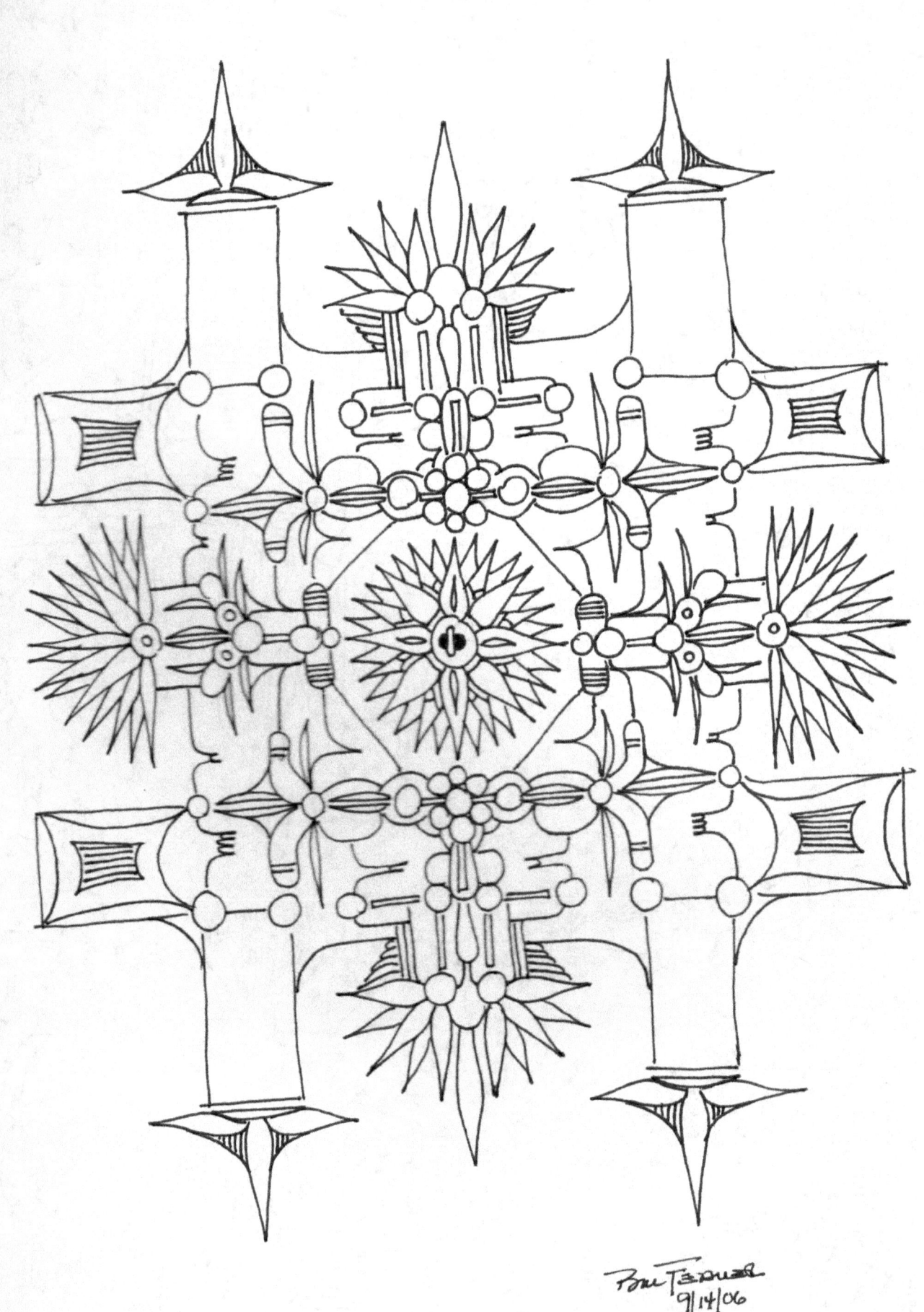

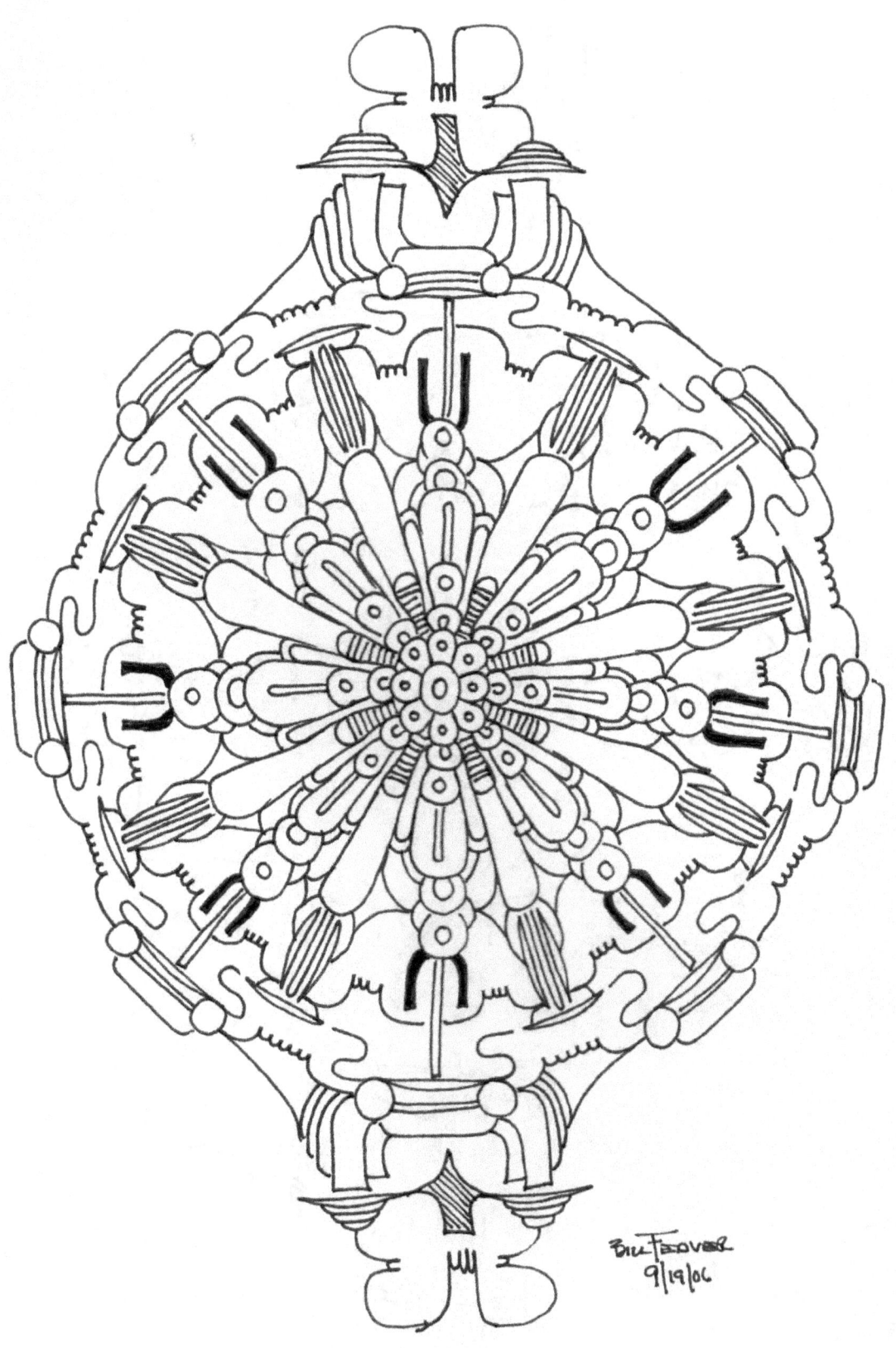

Bill Feaver
9/19/06

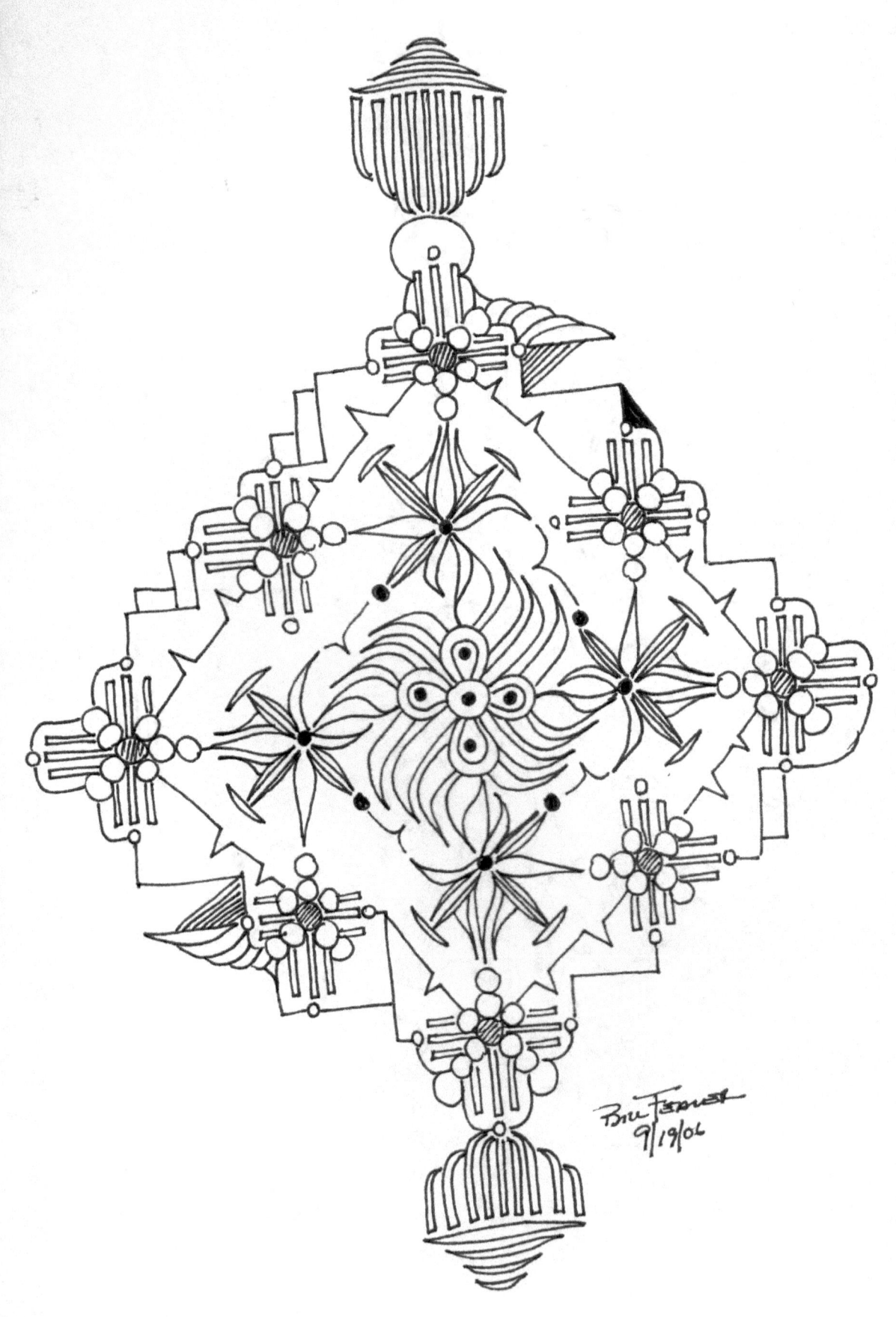

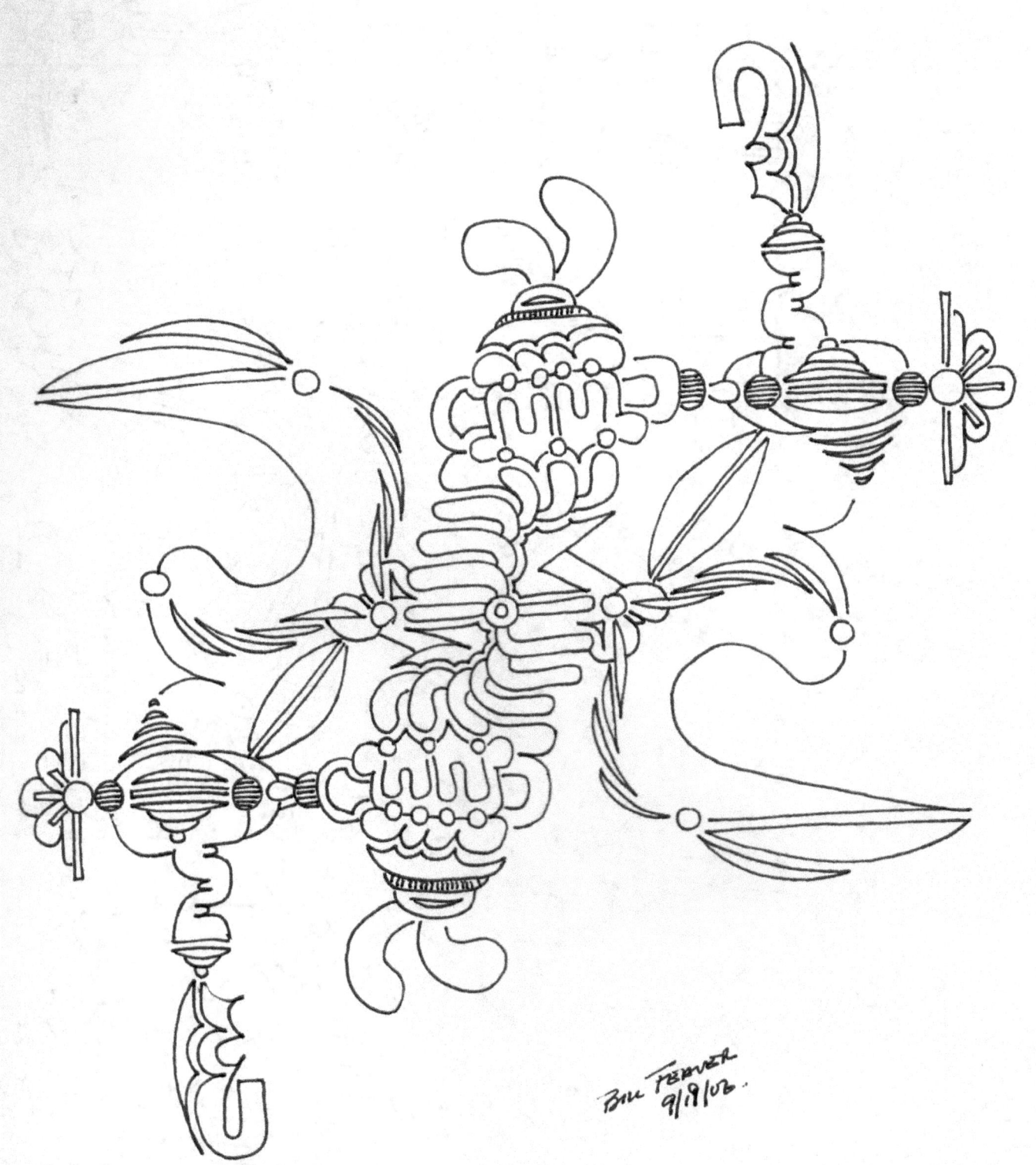

Bill Feaver
9/9/02

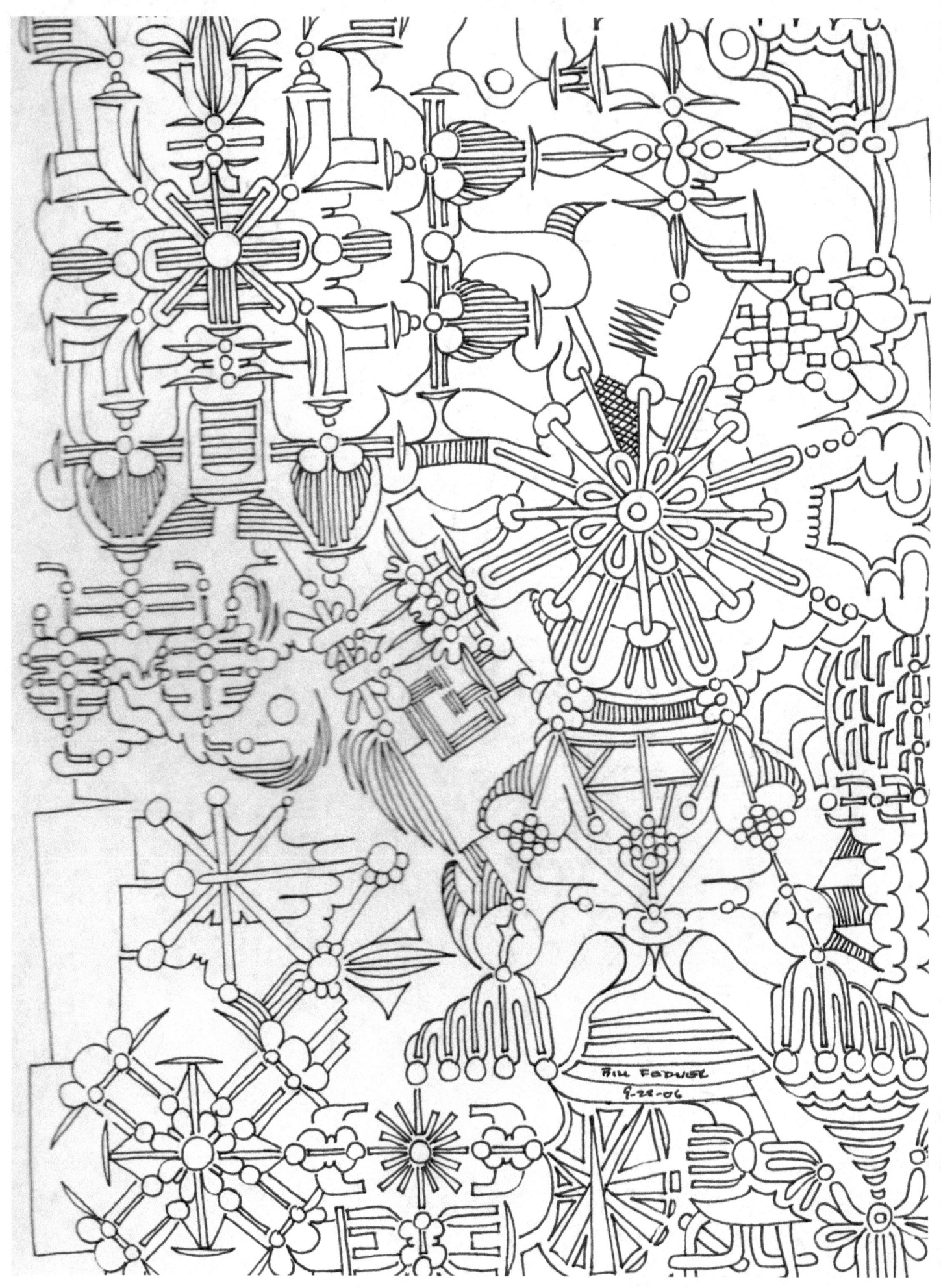

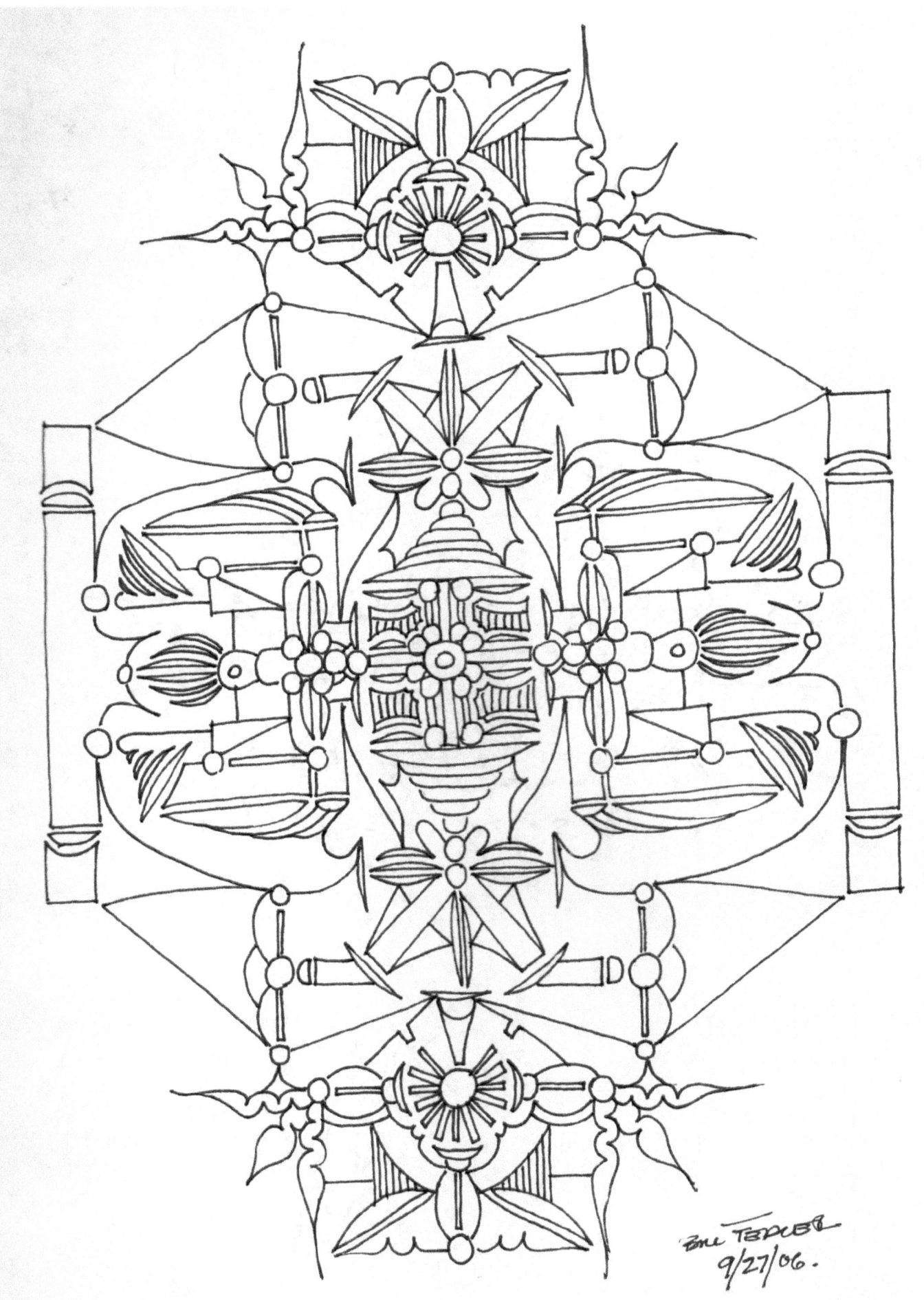

Bill Tepper
9/27/06.

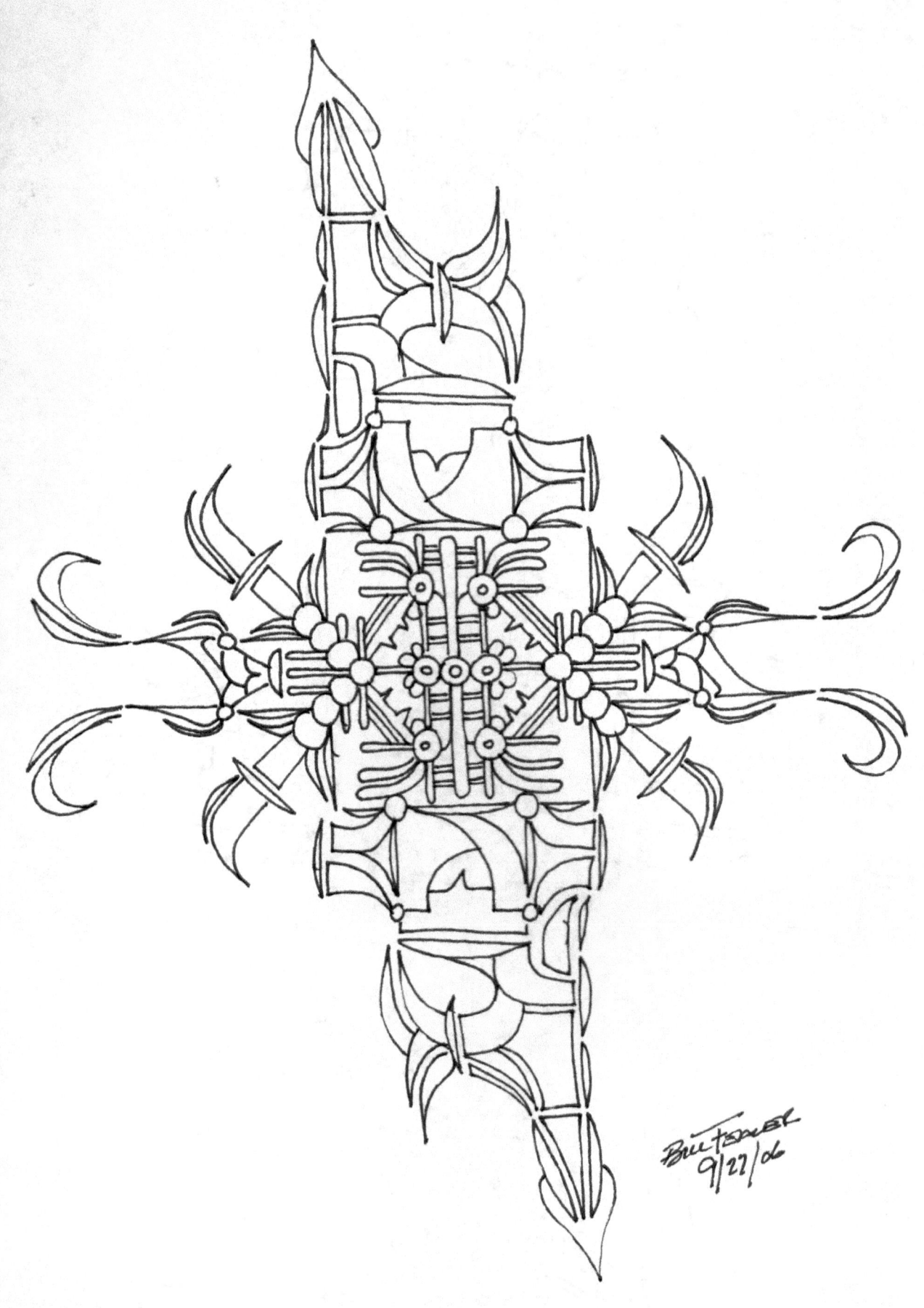

Bill Fowler
9/27/06

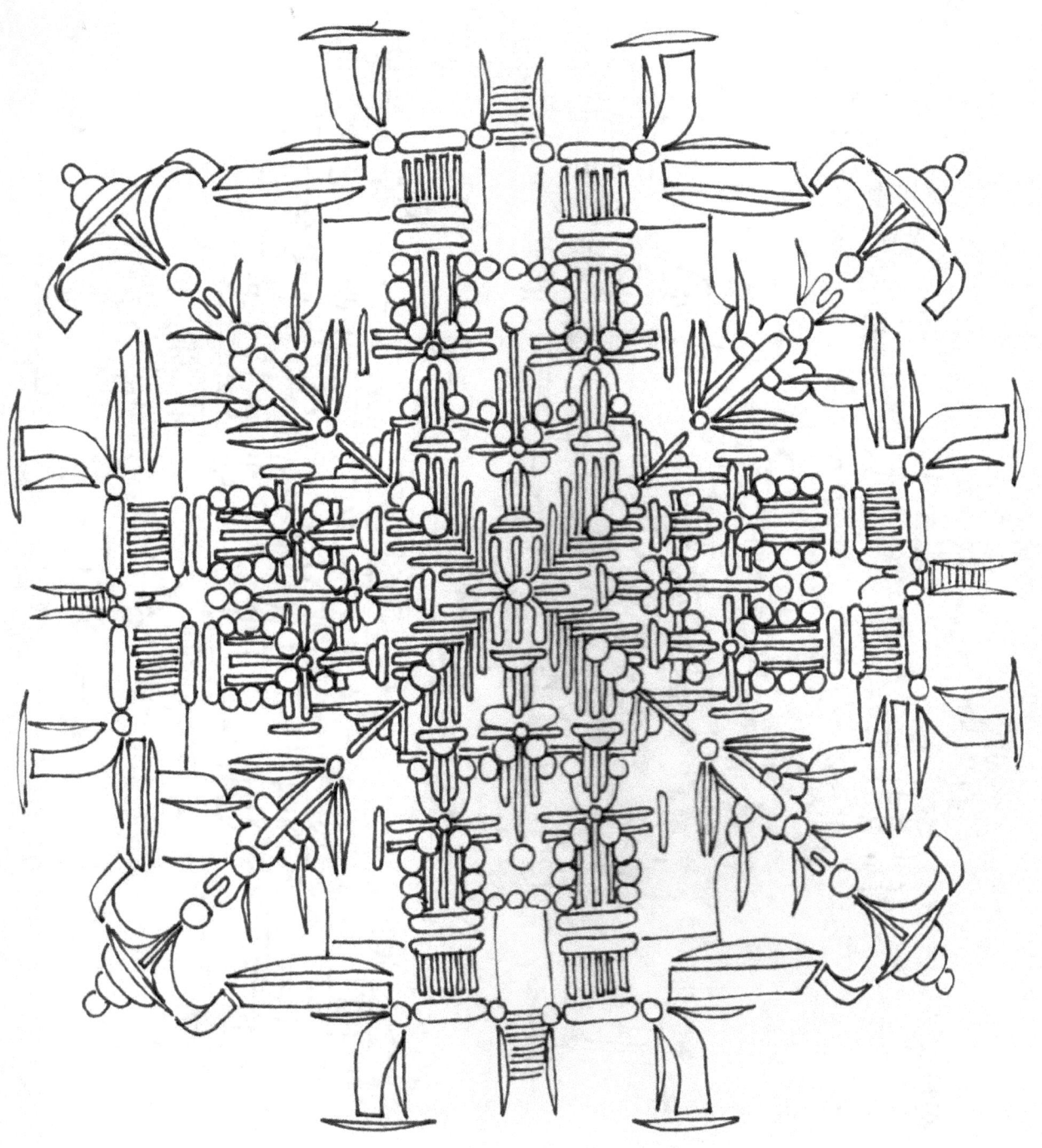

Bill Frazier
9/28/06

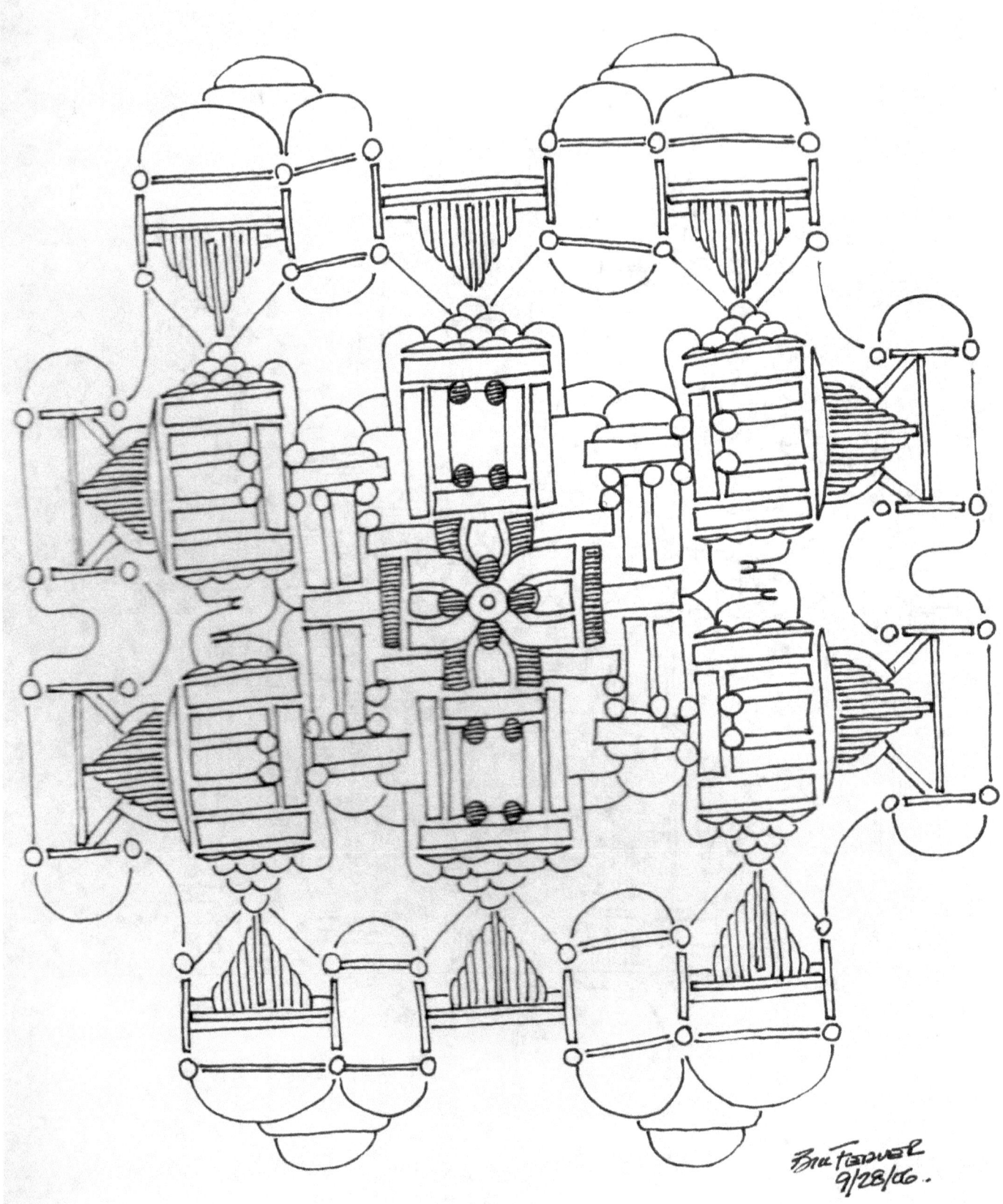

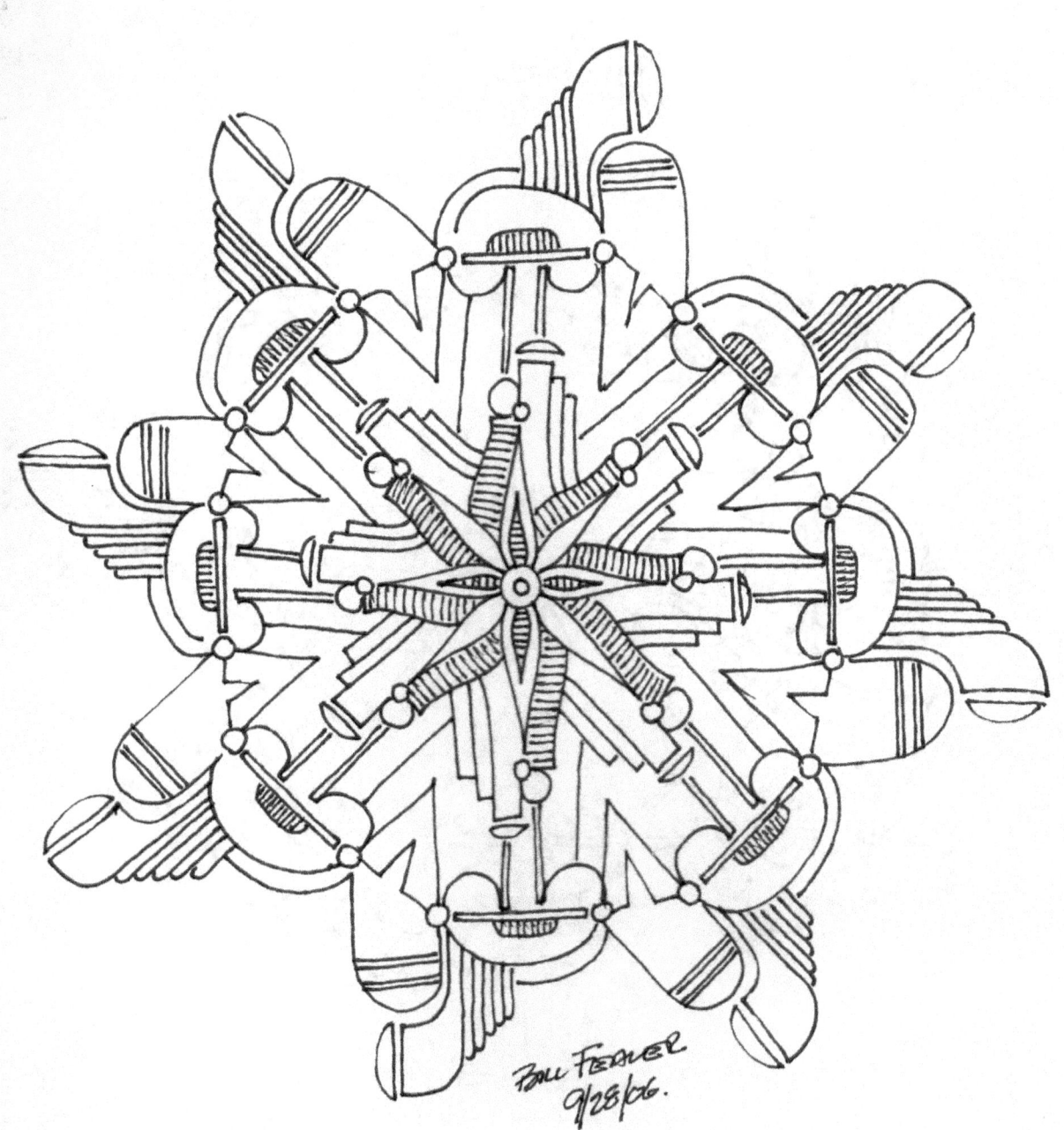

Bill Feaver
9/28/06.

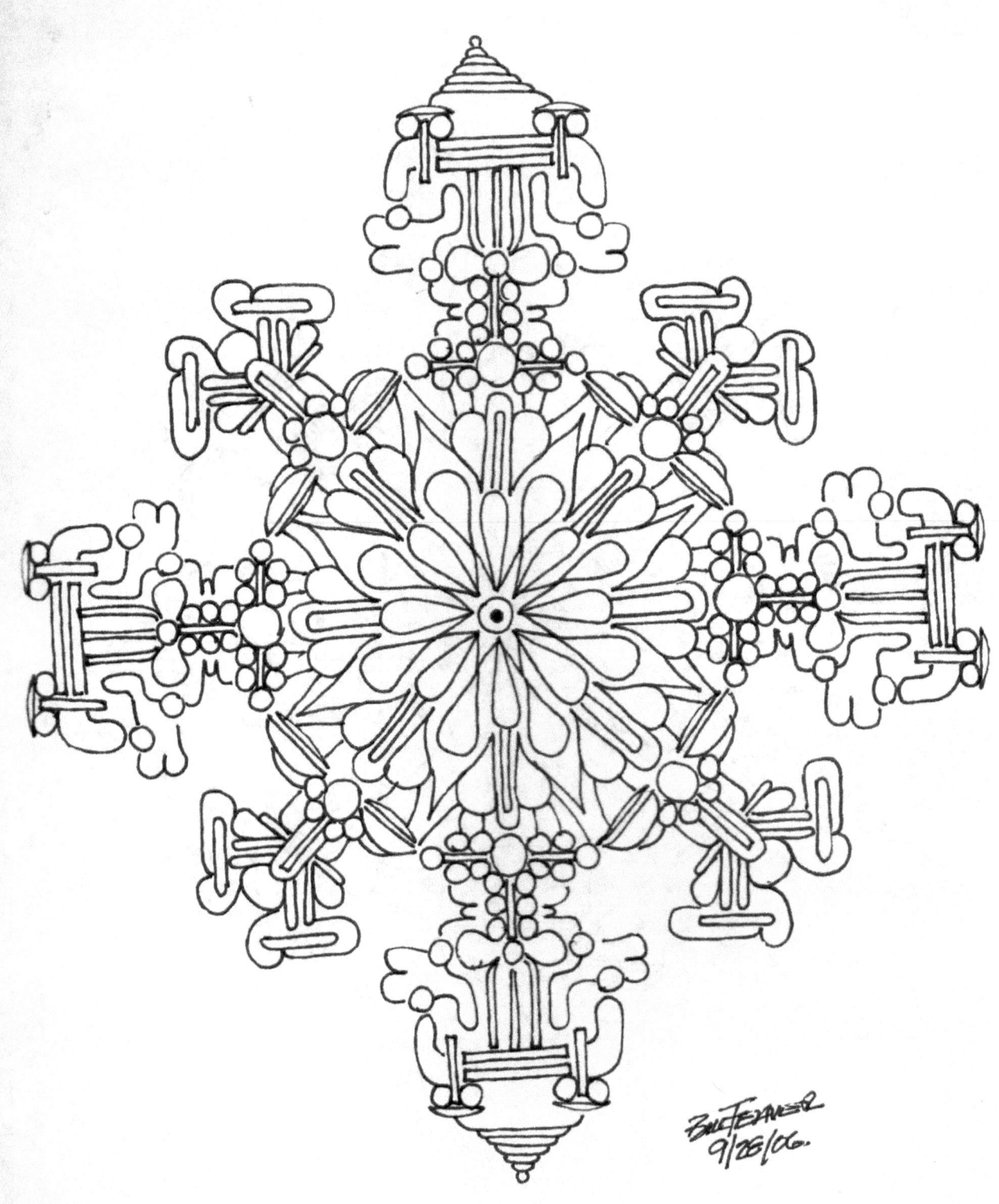

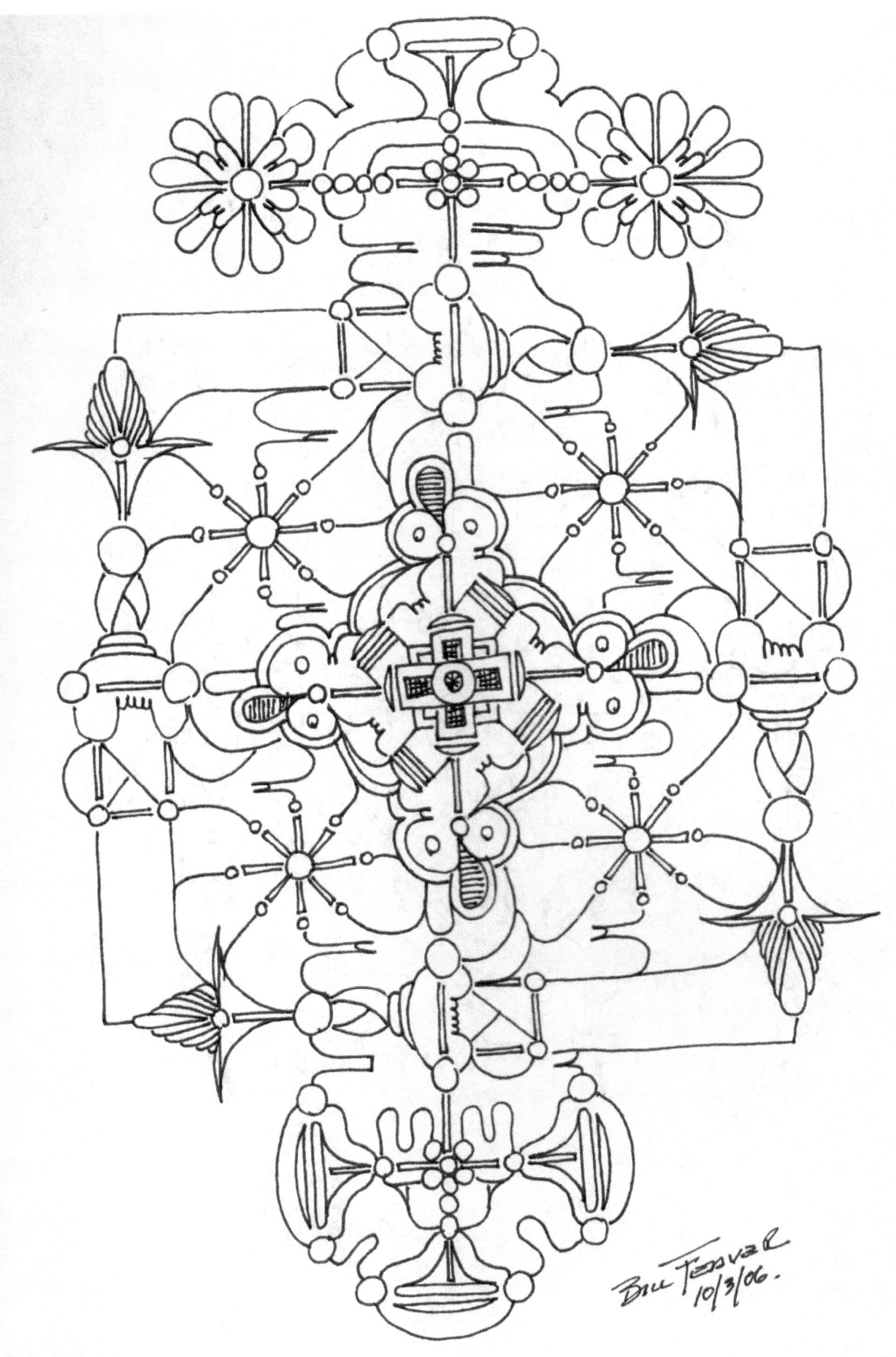

Bill Fessler
10/3/06.

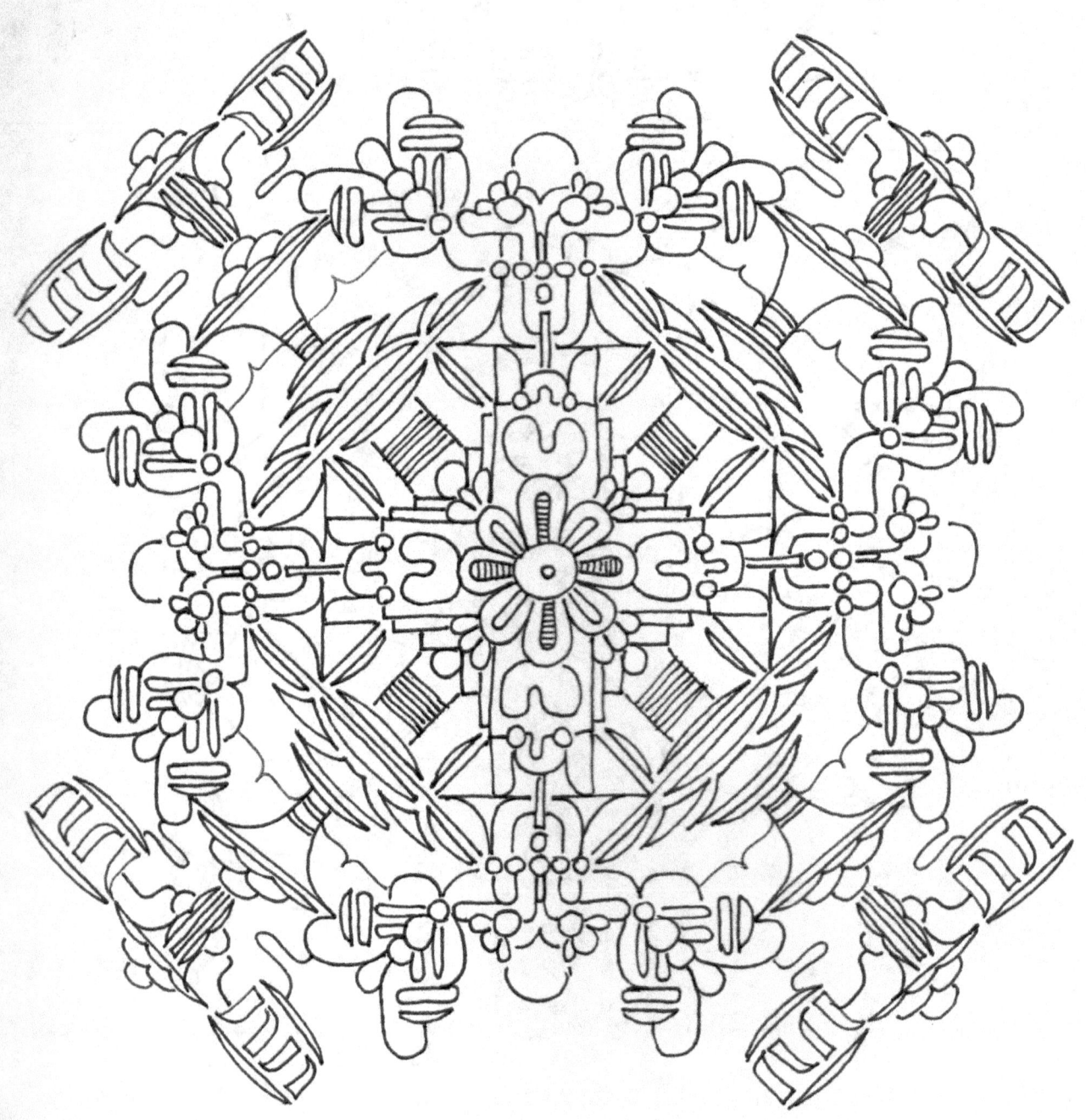

Bill Ferrell
19/04/06.

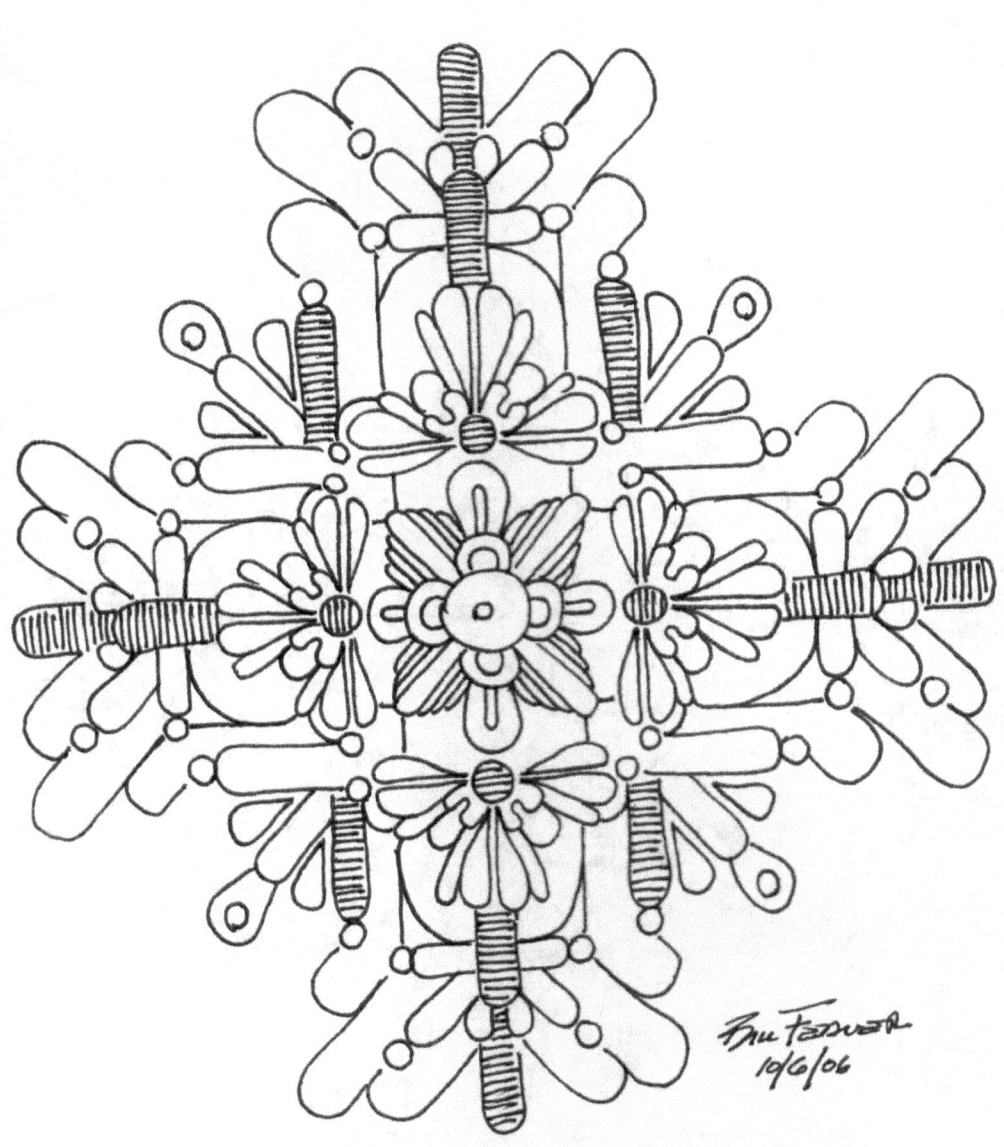

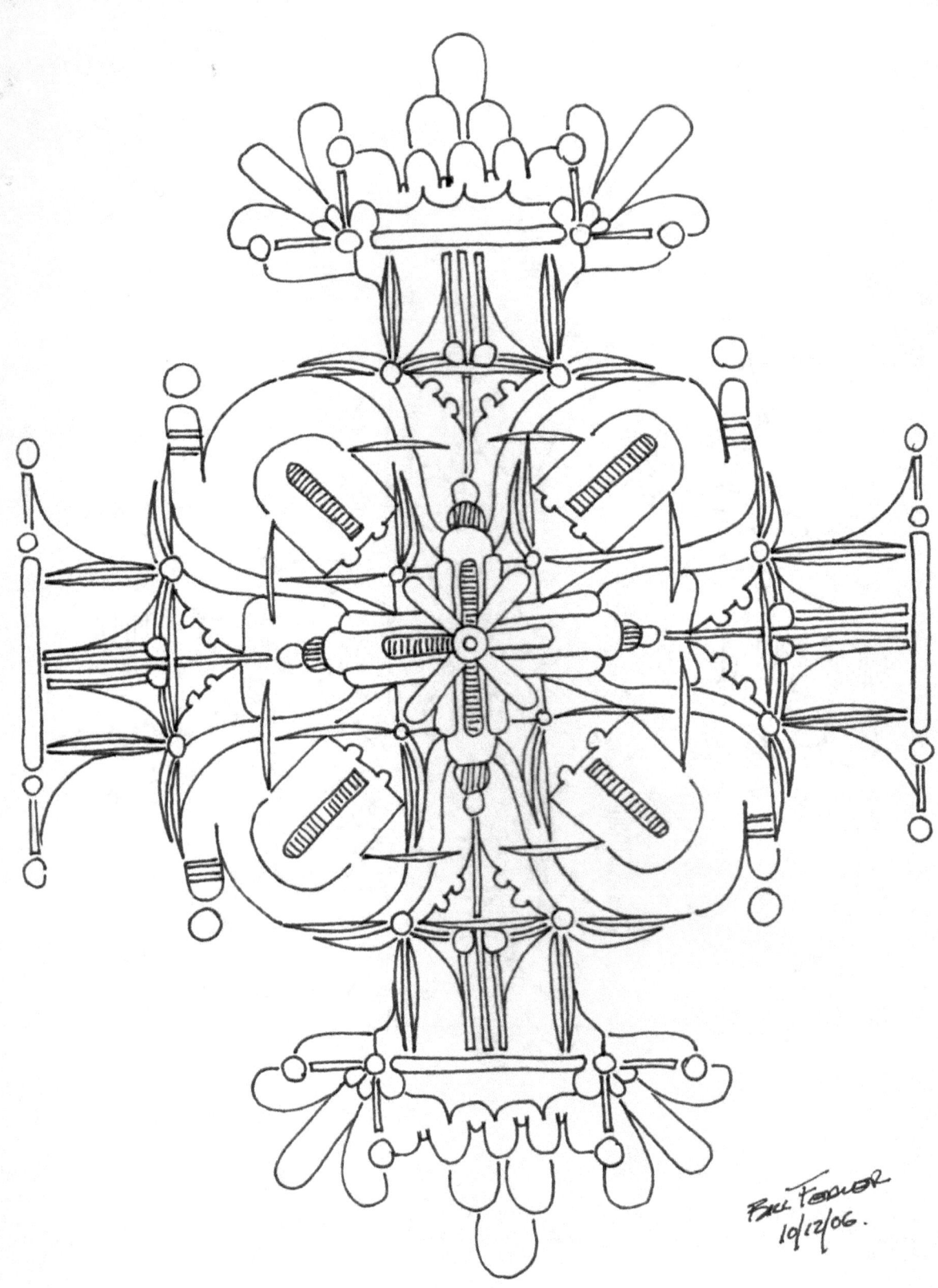

Bill Fermor
10/12/06.

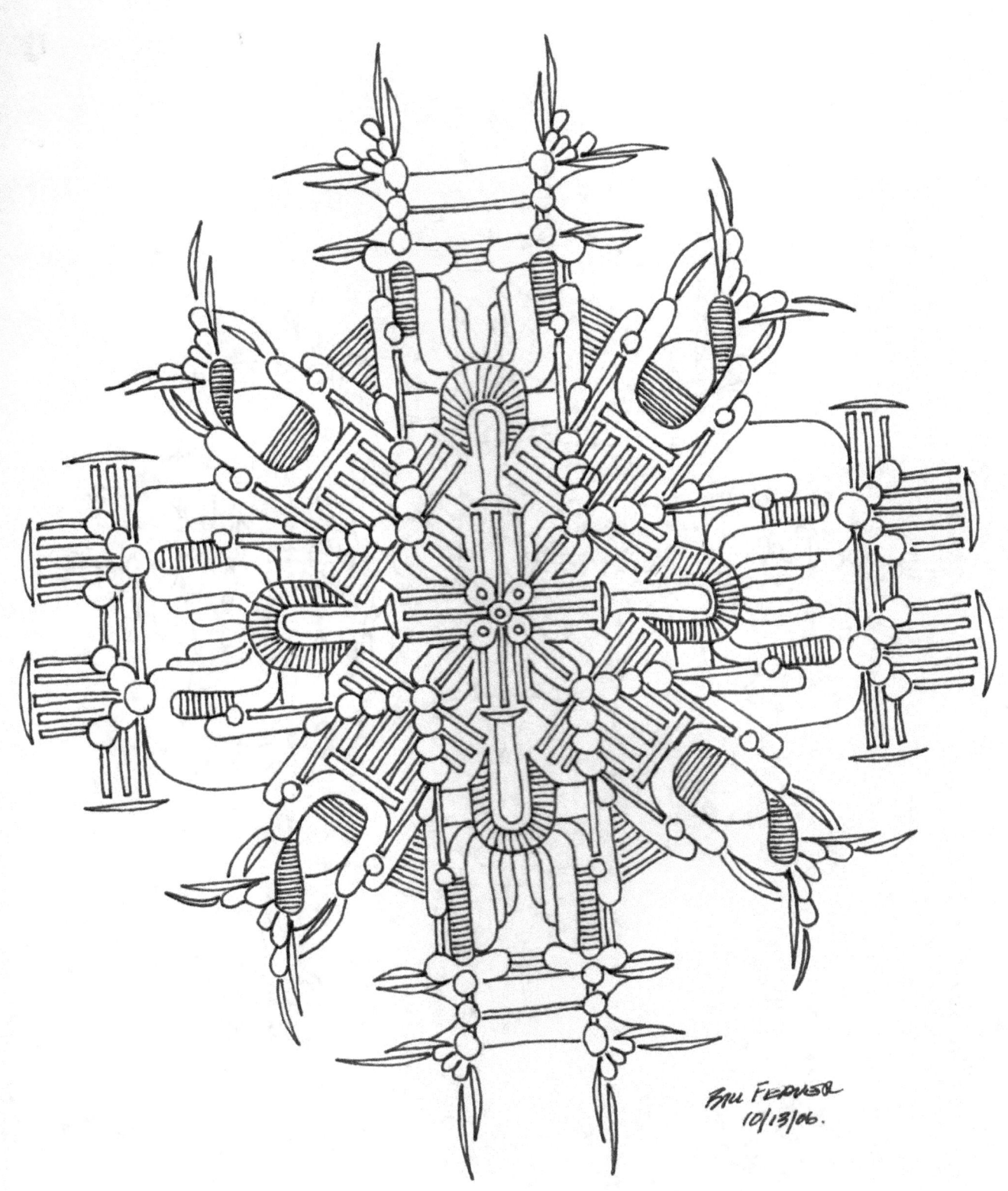

Bill Ferguson
10/13/06.

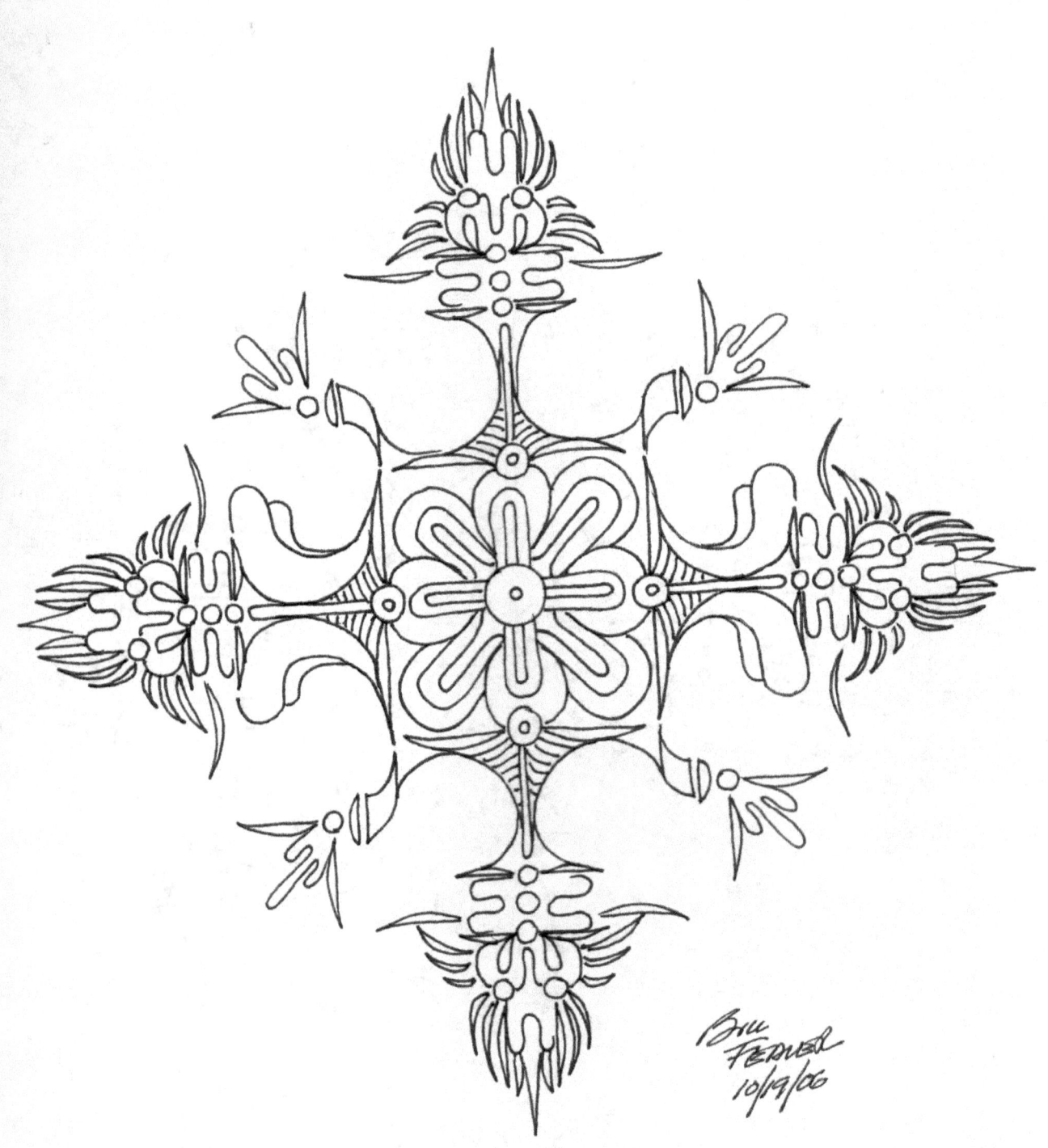

Bill
Ferner
10/19/06

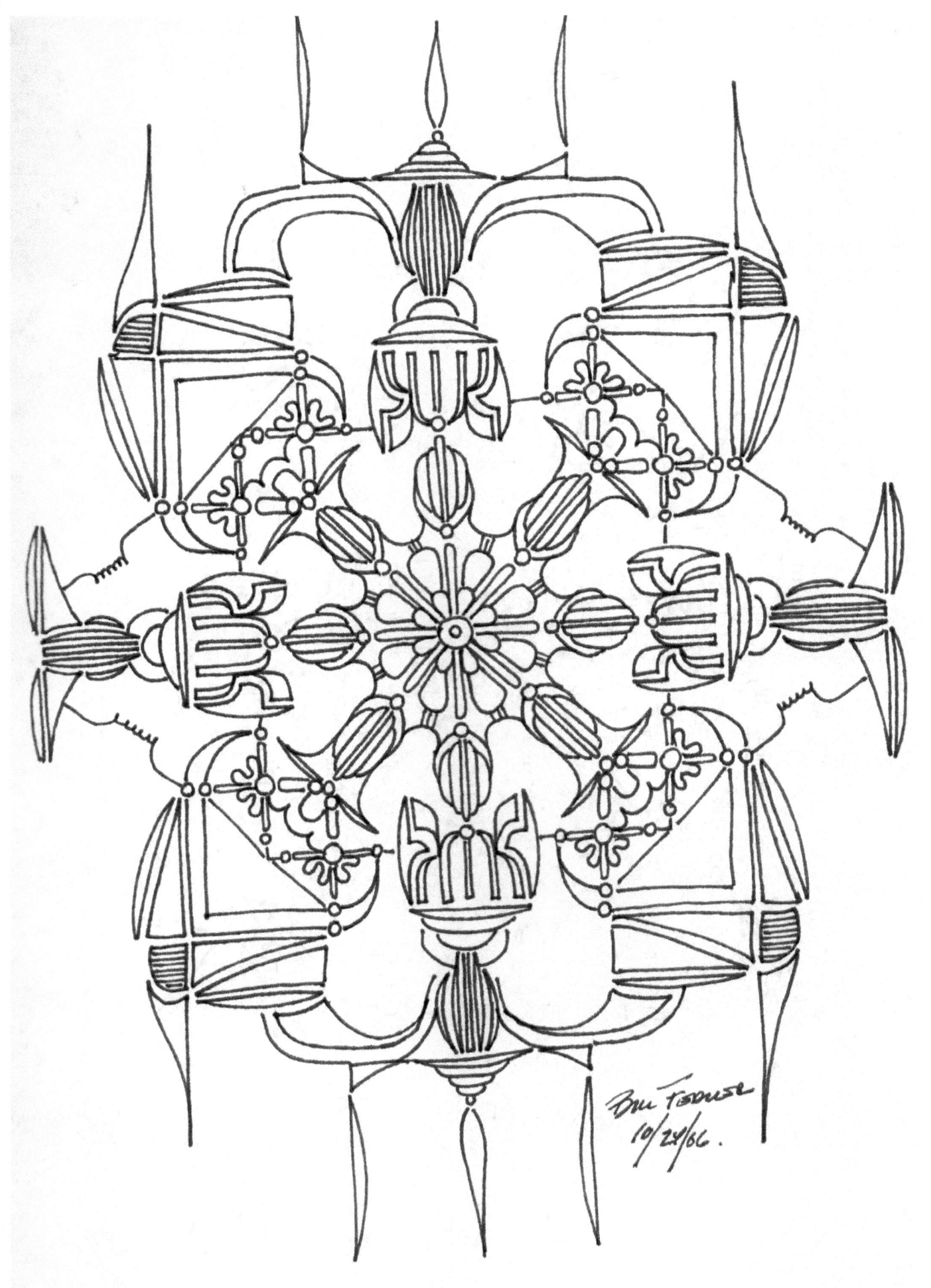

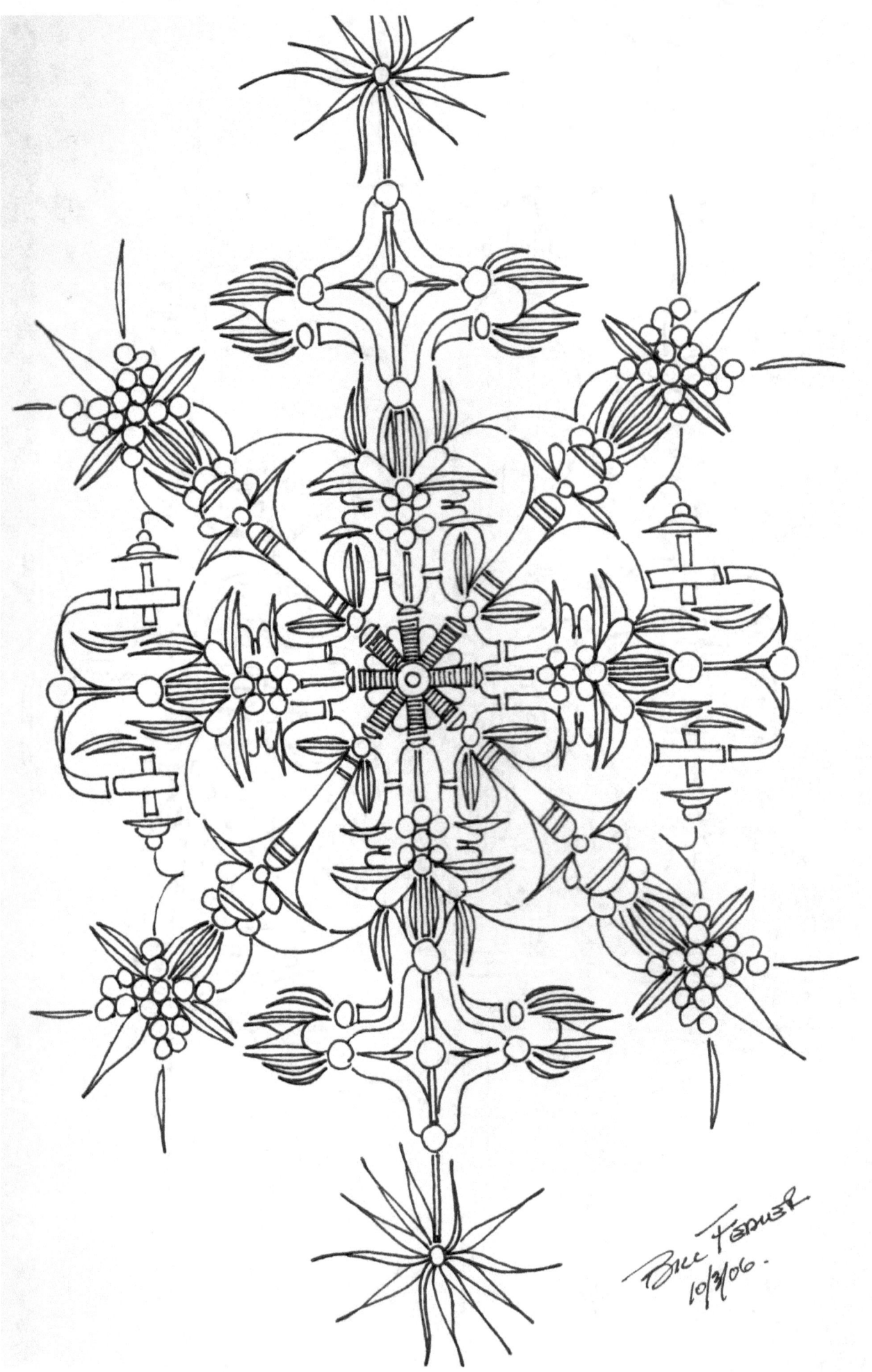

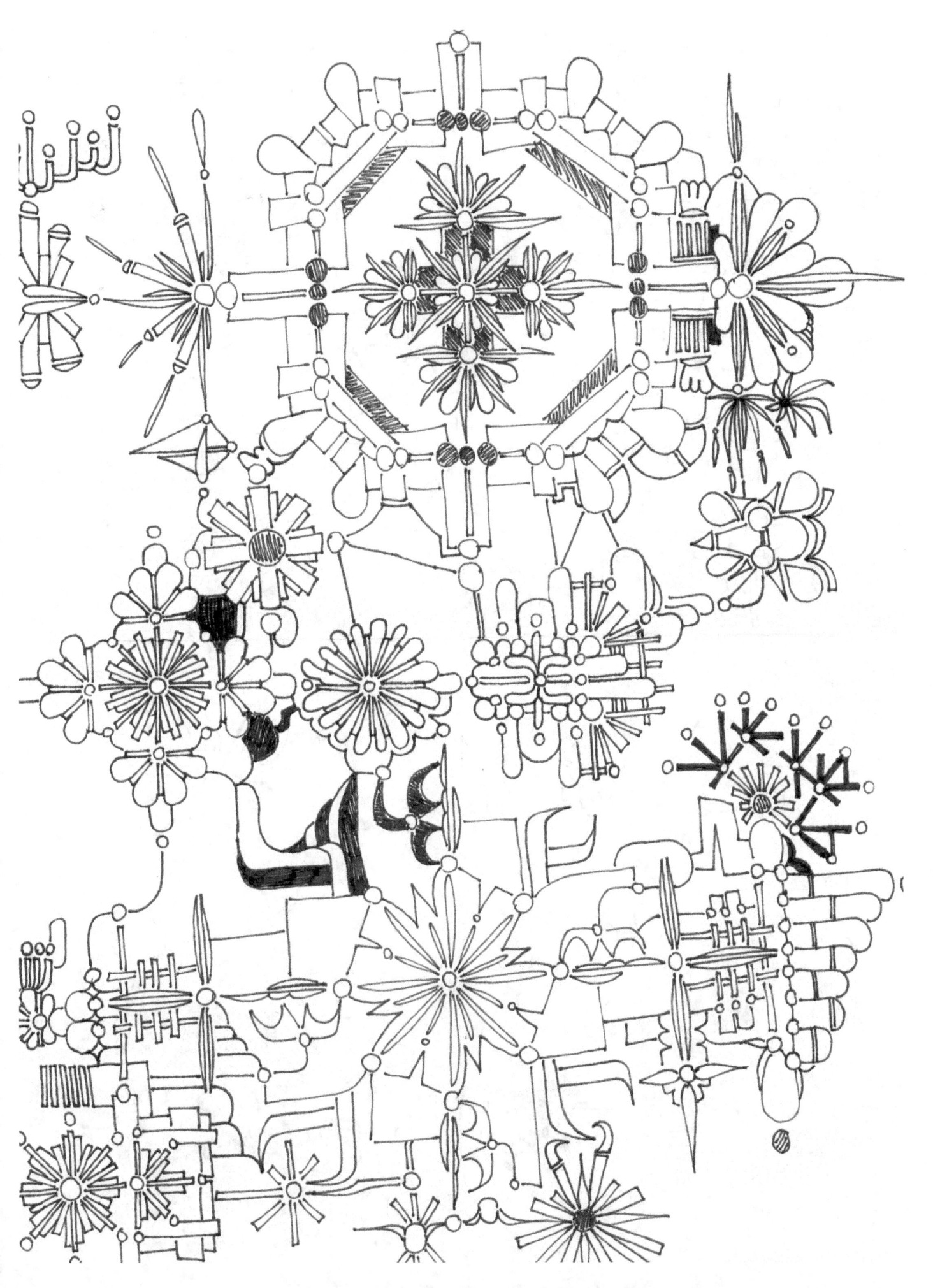

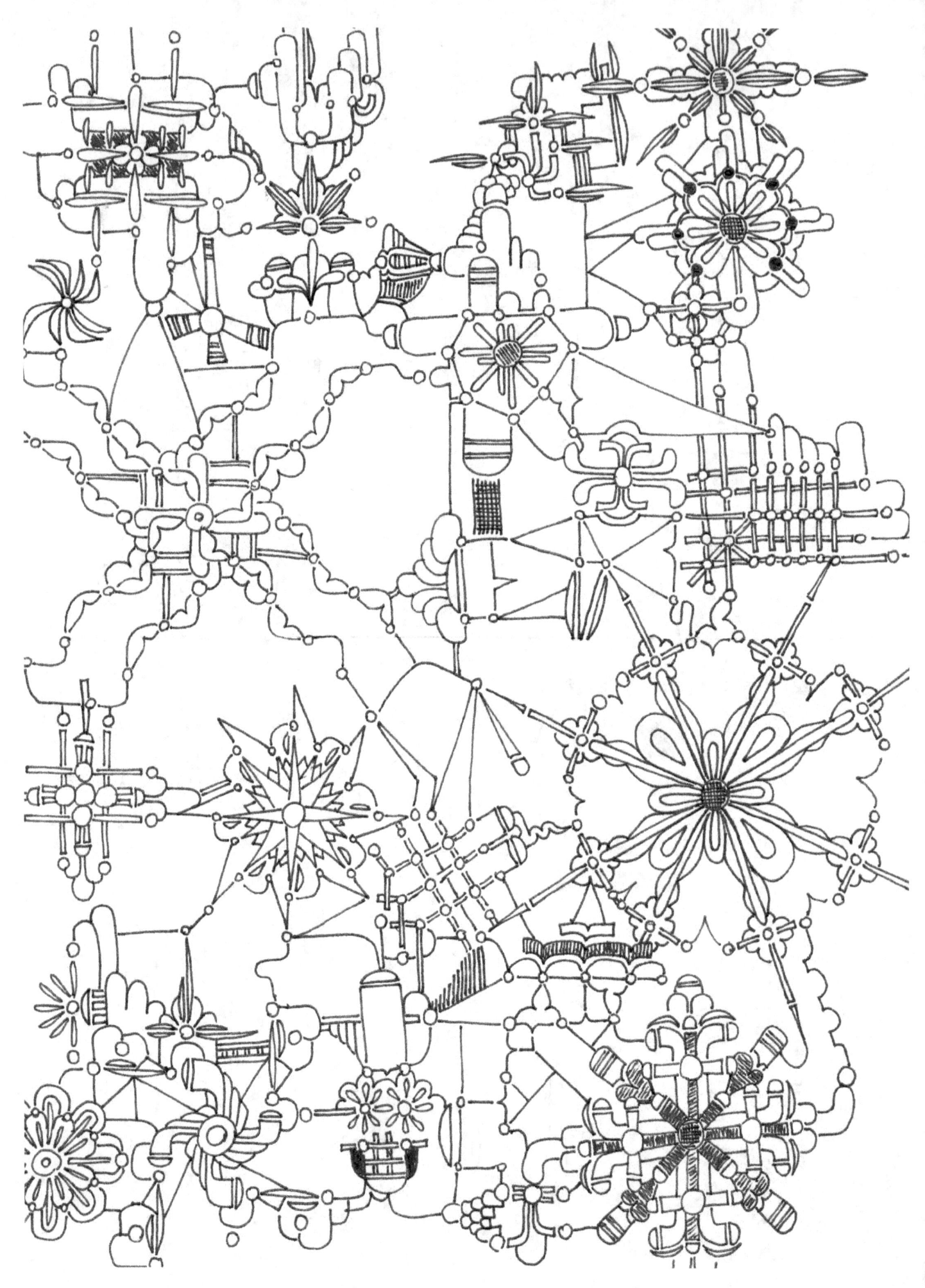

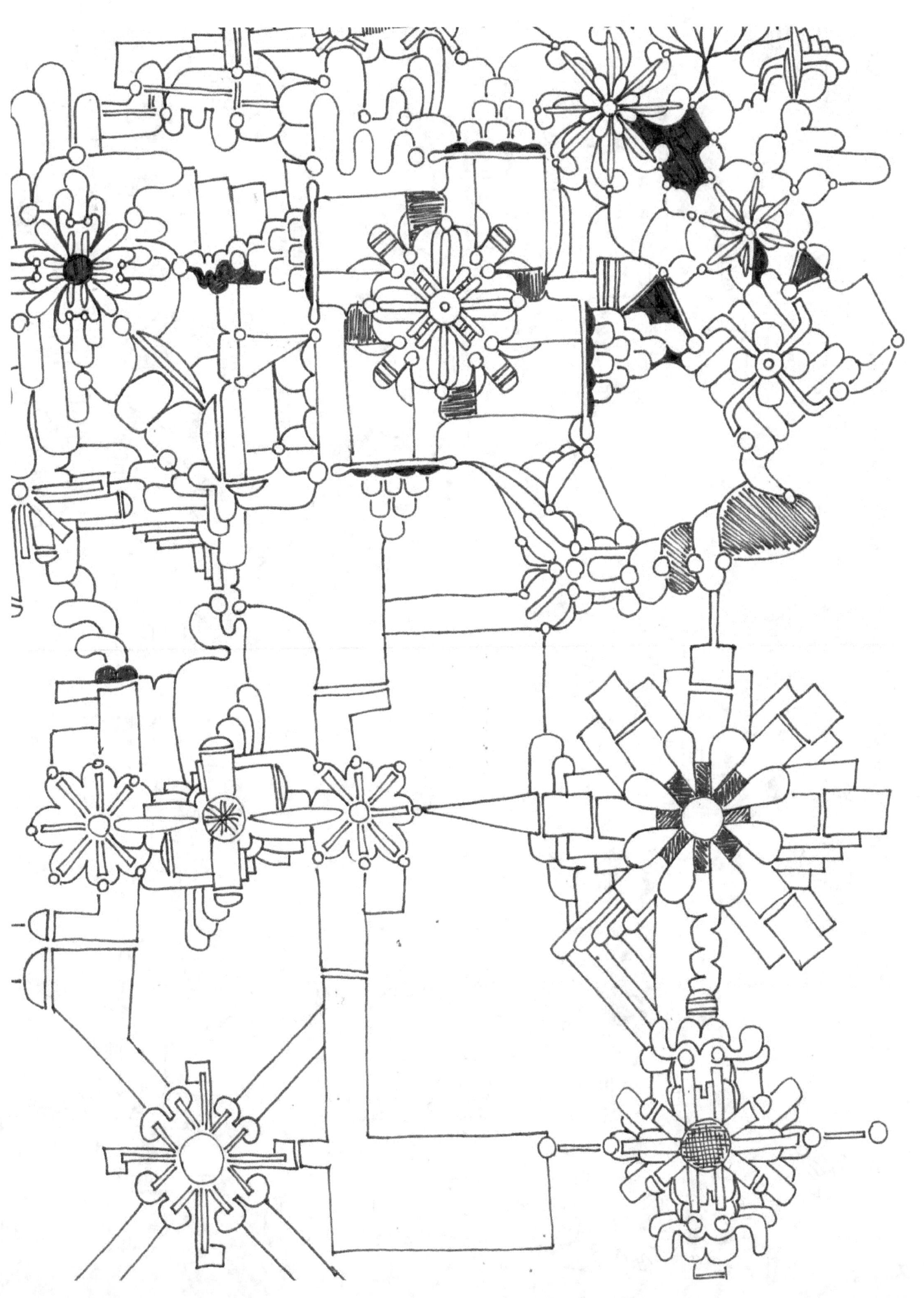

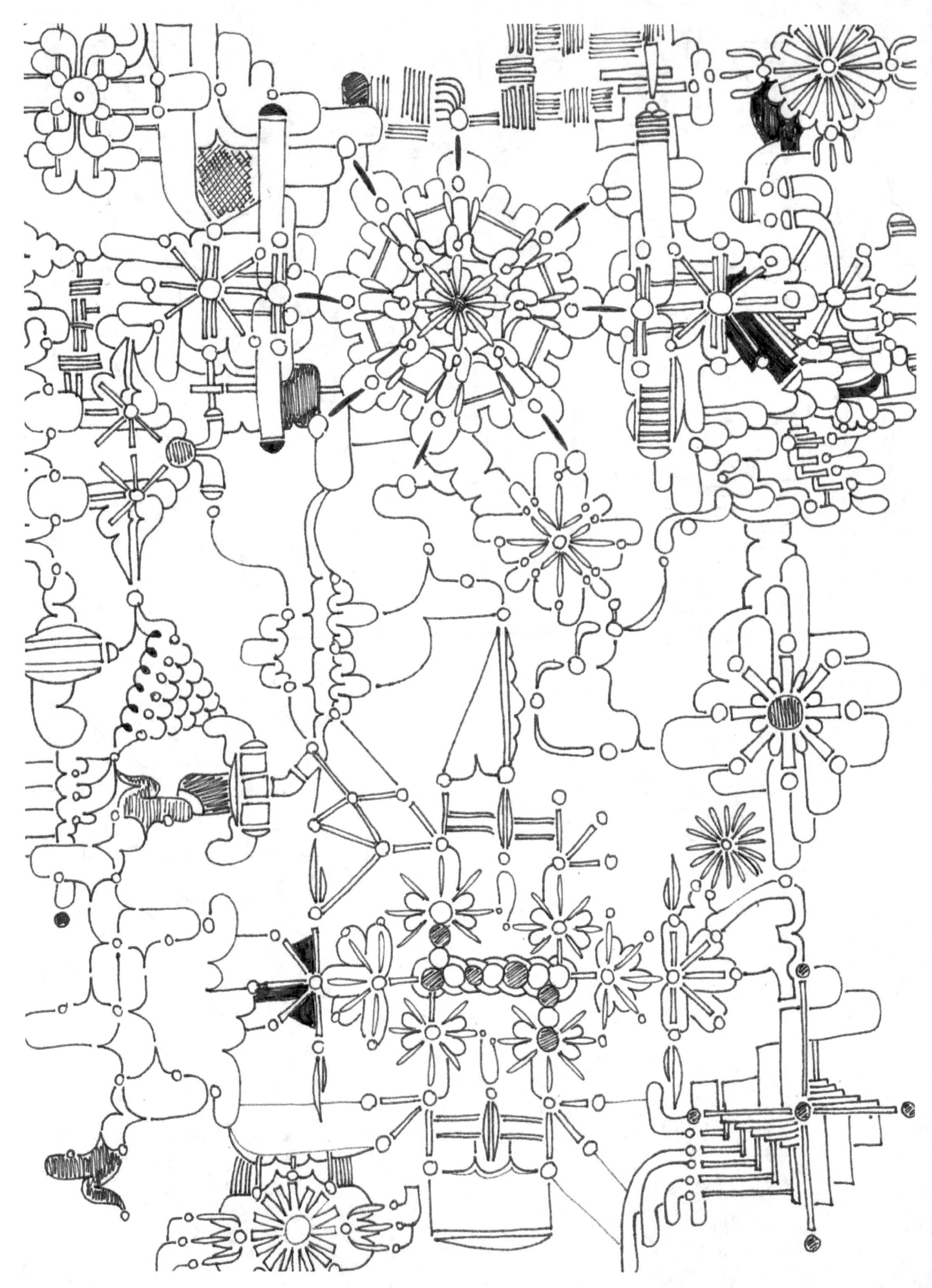

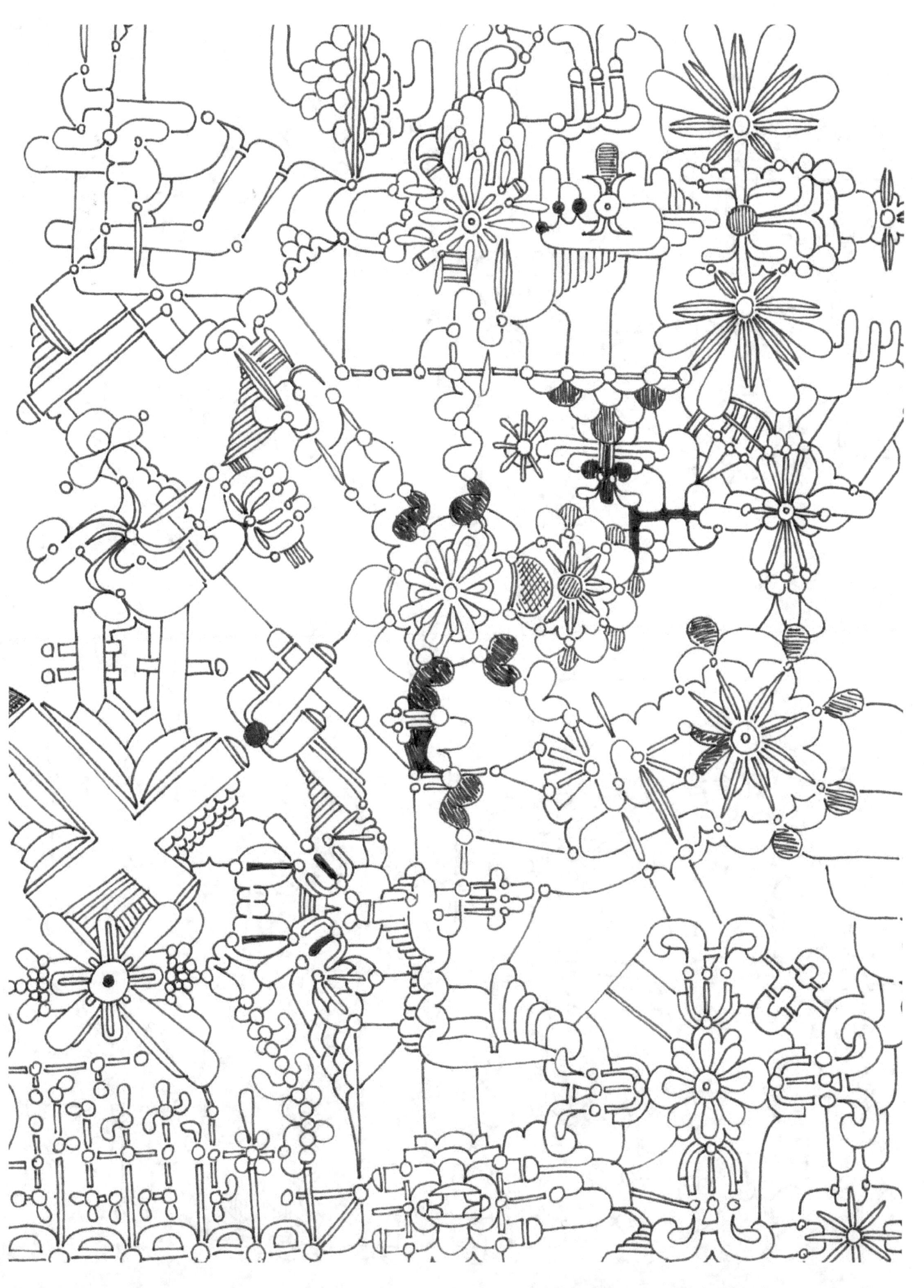

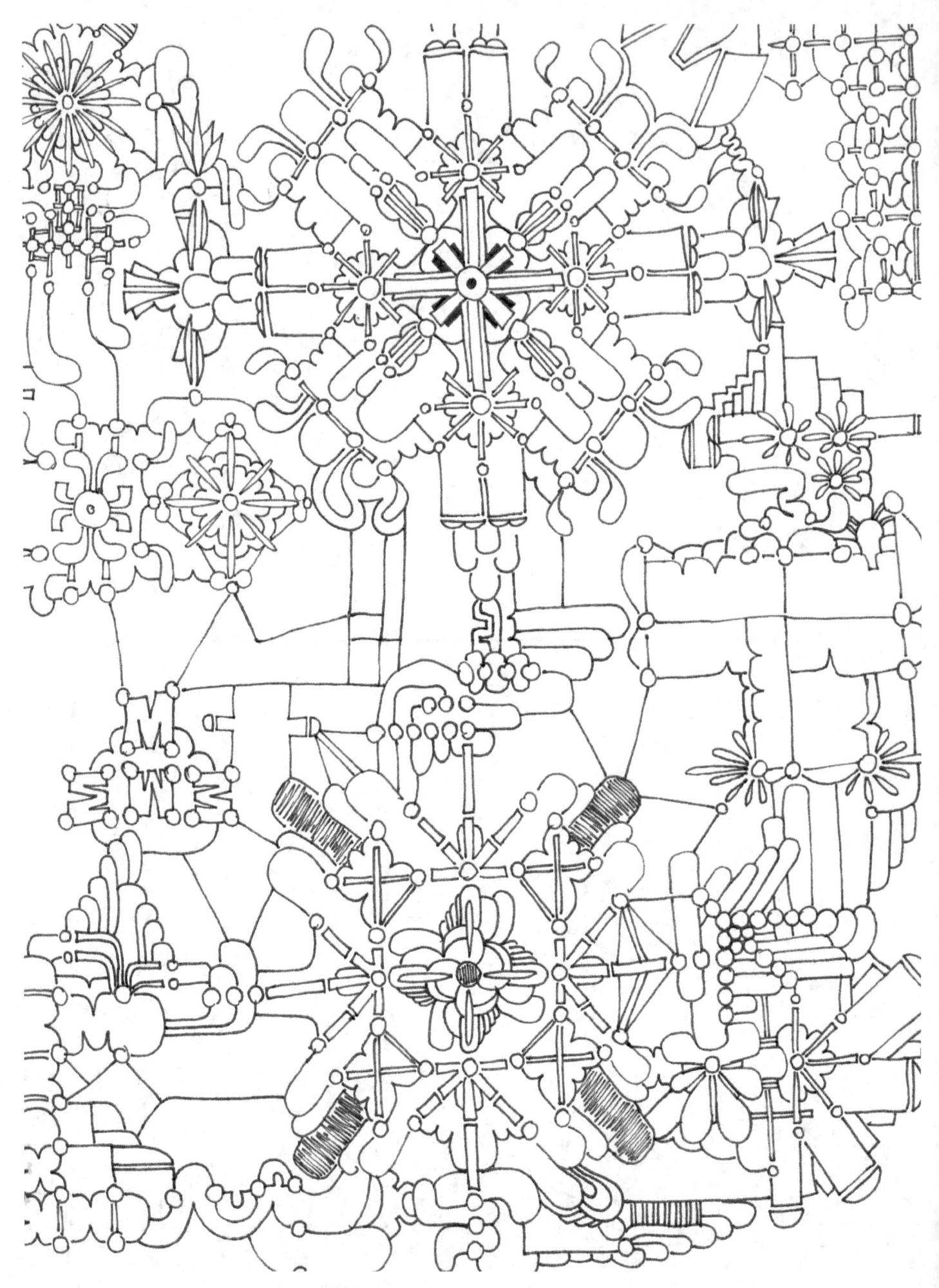